Agile

What You Need to Know About Agile Project Management, the Kanban Process, Lean Thinking, and Scrum

Contents

Introduction

Project management is the practice of guiding projects from their start to end while successfully achieving the project goals. Historical evidence suggests that project management has been in existence for centuries. Project management was limited to large and complex projects for a long time until businesses realized the need for smaller and simpler projects.

Different project management tools, methodologies, and frameworks have been introduced to help businesses and teams develop products and services successfully. However, every methodology, tool, and framework has its pros and cons. Traditional project management methodologies that were practiced until the 21st century were largely linear and sequential.

The limitations of such traditional project management methodologies often resulted in projects being late and costing more than estimated. There was an increasing demand for a new project management methodology in the software development industry to help teams deliver projects on time while adjusting to changing requirements of customers instead of avoiding them.

In February 2001, seventeen software development practitioners and experts gathered at a ski resort in Utah. The group would later go on to be known as The Agile Alliance. The outcome of the gathering was the introduction of the Agile Manifesto. This introduced four values and twelve principles that described a new project management methodology aimed at solving the challenges faced by the software development industry at the time.

Many software development companies embraced the core values and guiding principles. Smaller teams working on shorter development cycles, while regularly receiving feedback from customers, enabled projects to be more open toward change instead of avoiding it. Self-organizing and cross-functional teams made projects easier to manage, while team members took ownership of their increased productivity.

The software development industry embraced Agile, and it was not long before other industries started experimenting with Agile values and principles. Although Agile was intended for software developments, its values and principles could be applied to any team environment irrespective of the industry or the type of product or service they were developing. As a result, Agile methodology is increasingly used in many different industries with great success.

Scrum is an Agile framework that enables companies to adopt the Agile way of thinking without investing in prior experience and knowledge in Agile practices. While Agile does not provide steps to implement it, the Scrum framework provides clear steps on how to adopt Scrum practices making it easier for teams to adopt Agile.

The Scrum framework defines team roles, ceremonies, and artifacts that make it easier to adopt. Specific roles are given various responsibilities while Scrum ceremonies ensure that Agile principles of face-to-face interactions—providing customers with incremental versions of the product—and continuously improving as a team are achieved. Scrum artifacts provide the necessary documentation teams need; however, Agile methodology does not focus too much on documentation compared to traditional project management approaches.

The Kanban Method has its rules going all the way back to the Toyota factories in Japan, where it helped Toyota achieve high levels of productivity while reducing costs related to maintaining additional inventory. The Kanban method focuses on limiting *work in progress* where teams are encouraged to finish what they are working on before committing to new work. Teams are also encouraged to improve gradually, making Kanban very similar to the Agile way of thinking.

Lean Thinking is another philosophy that has many similarities to the Agile methodology. It focuses on helping processes increase productivity and profitability by reducing and eliminating wastes. Lean Thinking describes five principles that can be used to reduce and eliminate eight wastes resulting in the best use of resources. Lean Management has proven successful across several sectors and has fast become popular among many modern businesses.

Agile is a groundbreaking methodology that enabled teams to approach product development in an entirely different manner. It was able to solve many problems that the software development world was facing at the time and proved useful in many other sectors later on. Frameworks and methods such as Scrum, Kanban, and Lean share many similarities to Agile values and principles, but they are not the same. Agile, Scrum, Kanban, and Lean practices can be applied to different team environments depending on the projects, types of teams, and expectations involved to achieve project goals successfully.

Chapter 1: An Introduction to Project Management

Project management comprises time-sensitive goals assigned to a specific team and includes initiation, planning, execution, control, and closure of the project. Teams the world over, and across different sectors, use project management to achieve project-related goals with time constraints and predefined success criteria. These time constraints and success criteria are usually defined before the commencement of a particular project.

Scope, quality, time, and budget are the primary or key constraints of project management. In other words, the success of a project is gauged largely by how well it aligns with its expected or planned scope, quality, time, and budget. These constraints include the client's requirements and expectations and those of the company or organization the project team belongs to.

Client requirements and expectations are usually gathered and documented before a project begins. A clear understanding of those expectations and requirements enables the project stakeholders to form the project team that will create the end product to meet the predefined client requirements and expectations. Therefore, proper gathering and analysis of client requirements and expectations play a key role in determining a project's success.

A project is a temporary mission that is enforced to achieve a set of objectives during a specified period. Therefore, a project must have clear objectives regarding the product or service it will achieve. Furthermore, a project must also have a start and end date.

A project can create or make improvements to an existing product or service. A project can also be a one-time endeavor or an ongoing one. However, since a project needs to have a start and end date, an ongoing project is technically a project that repeats itself upon completion of its objectives.

For example, there may be a project where the objective is to manufacture a sports car according to strict guidelines in a month. The project team may complete the car in 29 days, bringing it to a closure. The same team might move on to the next project, which is the same: manufacturing the same car with the same requirements and time frame. Such projects are called ongoing projects.

Project management aims to utilize the resources available to a team to achieve project objectives without delays and to exceed the budget. The planning of resources includes personnel, finances, technology, and intellectual property. Project management also aims to meet predefined customer requirements and expectations while also facilitating some changes to those requirements and expectations along the way.

A project manager's job is to use a suitable project management methodology to initiate, plan, execute, control, and close the project within the allowed time frame. In most methodologies, the project manager determines when certain project components will be completed and which team members will contribute to those tasks. Some project management methodologies involve smaller teams making those decisions and initiating and executing tasks.

1.1 History of Project Management

Ancient records prove that officials were allocated management roles to complete different sections of the Great Pyramid of Giza built by the Pharaohs. The construction of the four faces of the Great Pyramid was assigned to different managers, who ensured they were completed on time. This would have involved planning, execution, and control.

The Great Wall of China is another enormous project that would have required a lot of management skills. Historical data indicate that the laborers were divided into three main groups or categories: soldiers, commoners, and criminals. These groups—that amounted to millions of people—were separately managed. Therefore, there is concrete evidence suggesting that some project management levels have been around for thousands of years.

The civil engineering industry in the 1950s first applied project management practices; however, they were limited to complex projects. The practices were not applied for smaller projects at the time. Over the next decade, project management expanded into many other engineering fields.

Henry Laurence Gantt, an American mechanical engineer who created the Gantt Chart in 1917, was one of the pioneers of scientific management and project management practices. Gantt charts became popular as a tool to guide projects, and he introduced many other techniques and tools to help plan and control projects. Henri Fayol, a French engineer, also introduced the five project management functions, which laid a foundation for project management for years to come.

The era of modern project management dawned in the 1950s, with many core engineering fields contributing towards its evolution. Project management was recognized as an important practice and discipline in many engineering sectors around this time. Gantt charts were used to manage most projects along with various informal tools before the 1950s. However, two project scheduling models emerged around this time that changed how project management was carried out.

This Critical Path Method (CPM) was one of those mathematical methods. It was developed through a joint venture between the Remington Rand Corporation and the DuPont Corporation. CPM quickly gained popularity and was used to manage plant maintenance projects.

The Program Evaluation and Review Technique (PERT) was the other project scheduling model that emerged. It was a model created by the U.S. Navy Special Projects Office along with Booz Allen Hamilton and the Lockheed Corporation for the Polaris missile submarine program. CPM and PERT have many similarities; however, they have numerous distinctions that make them more or less suitable for certain projects or industries.

CPM was used to manage projects that have predefined time frames for different tasks. PERT, on the other hand, was widely used in projects with uncertain time frames. Many private entities across different industries quickly started using CPM and PERT to manage different projects depending on their characteristics.

Different techniques were introduced to estimate and manage the cost of projects with Hans Lang dominating the way. The American Association of Cost Engineers was formed in 1956 by individuals and companies that used different project management tools and methodologies. The organization is now known as the Association for the Advancement of Cost Engineering (AACE). Practices that involve planning, cost estimation, scheduling, cost control, and project control have, for decades, been guided by the AACE.

The United States Department of Defense developed the concept of the Work Breakdown Structure (WBS) for the Polaris ballistic missile project. It was published upon completion of the project and mandated for use in future projects of the same size and scope. The WBS is a hierarchical structure for tasks and deliverables that need to be completed to close a particular project. The method was later adopted by the private sector and remains to be a highly useful project management tool to this date.

The International Project Management Association (IPMA) was formed in Vienna in 1965. It acted as a forum for project managers to share information, with more than 50 project management associations from across the world joining its network. The IPMA intends to develop the profession of project management with its membership exceeding 120,000 in 2012.

The Project Management Institute (PMI), formed in 1969 in the United States, aimed to improve the science, practice, and profession of project management. PMI's first symposium was held in Atlanta, Georgia, the same year with 83 attendees. Since then, the institute has taken giant strides by being highly recognized around the world for publishing *A Guide to the Project Management Body of Knowledge (PMBOK),* which acts as an essential tool for project managers. It includes different project management practices suitable for "most projects, most of the time."

The Project Management Institute also began issuing certifications for project management experts that highly contributed to the worldwide recognition of project management as a profession and expertise. PMI's two project management certifications are Project Management Professional (PMP) and Certified Associate in Project Management (CAPM).

Simpact Systems Limited created PROMPT II in 1975 as a response to the outcry for a solution to address projects extending delivery dates and exceeding budgets, especially in the IT industry. PROMPTII sets guidelines to the way stages flow in a computer project. The Government's Central Computing and Telecommunications Agency (CCTA) in the United Kingdom adopted PROMPT II for all of its information systems projects in 1979.

Author, philosopher, and business leader, Dr. Eliyahu M. Goldratt, introduced the Theory of Constraints (TOC) in his novel *The Goal* in 1984. The management philosophy was aimed at helping companies continuously achieve their goals. The theory aims to identify constraints that limit projects from achieving their goals. The process uses Five Focusing steps to restructure an organization around the constraints that are identified. The algorithms and philosophy behind TOC laid the foundation for the development of Critical Chain Project Management.

Scrum was recognized as a project management style in a paper titled "The New New Product Development Game," written by professors Hirotaka Takeuchi and Ikujiro Nonaka in 1986. Scrum was initially intended for the management of projects in software development. However, it later became popular as a general project management approach that was used in many different sectors.

Earned Value Management (EVM) was recognized as a project management technique only in the late 1980s and early 1990s; however, the concept has been used in factories since the dawn of the twentieth century. EVM became a key part of program management and procurement with the elevation of EVM leadership to the Undersecretary of Defense for Acquisition in 1989. EVM detected performance issues in the Navy McDonnell Douglas A-12 Avenger II program, which resulted in the program's cancellation by the Secretary of Defense, Dick Cheney, in 1991.

The PRojects IN Controlled Environments (PRINCE) method, developed from PROMPT II, was made the standard for all UK government information systems projects in 1989. However, PRINCE soon became known as a rigid approach that was only applicable to limited projects, such as larger ones.

Such limitations were addressed later in 1996 with the introduction of PRINCE2. While PRINCE was developed mainly for information technology and information systems projects, PRINCE2 was more generic. As a result, it was adopted by companies in many different sectors. PRINCE2 was also more applicable to projects of varying scales that contributed to its popularity.

Critical Chain Project Management (CCPM) was invented by Eliyahu M. Goldratt in 1997. It was based on algorithms and methods in Theory of Constraints (TOC) published by Goldratt in 1984. CCPM aims at maintaining even resources while ensuring flexibility when it comes to starting times of different tasks so that a project runs on schedule. PMBOK was recognized as a standard by the American National Standards Institute (ANSI) in 1998. The Institute of Electrical and Electronics Engineers (IEEE) also followed suit the same year.

Seventeen software experts gathered at The Lodge resort in Snowbird, Utah, in February 2001 to discuss and share knowledge regarding lightweight software development methodologies. This meet up resulted in the publication of the *Manifesto for Agile Software Development*. It defined the Agile approach, with some of the manifesto's authors going on to form the Agile Alliance, a non-profit organization focused on promoting software development in line with the twelve core principles introduced in the manifesto.

AACE International introduced the Total Cost Management Framework in 2006 that focused on applying the knowledge and skills of cost engineering. The fourth edition of the PMBOK Guide was released in 2008. A key revision of PRINCE2 took place in 2009, making the method more customizable and simpler. The updated method offers project managers seven principles to complete projects within budget, on time, and with the right quality.

The International Organization for Standardization in 2012 published *ISO 21500:2012, Guidance on Project Management*, as a result of work carried out over five years with contributions from experts from over 50 countries. The standard can be used by any organization, including private, public, or community, and any type of project irrespective of size, duration, and complexity.

The fifth edition of the PMBOK Guide was published in 2012. The fifth edition introduced characteristics and rules that are considered as good practice in project management. It also includes Project Stakeholder Management, the tenth knowledge area in the guide, and four new processes for planning.

Chapter 2: Agile Project Management

Agile is a project management approach that is flexible and modern. It allows the breaking down of larger projects into simpler and manageable tasks that are then completed in short iterations known as *sprints*. Agile allows a team to adapt to change and complete work quickly.

The Agile project management approach may sound difficult to manage and somewhat complex. However, most companies, teams, and project managers often practice many approaches and principles of Agile without knowing so. Therefore, adopting Agile may not be as difficult as it may seem.

Agile was developed to solve different challenges that software development projects were facing at the time of its inception. However, today, Agile is used to manage projects, not only in the field of information technology but construction, education, marketing, and more. Therefore, many companies can benefit from adopting Agile irrespective of the sector they belong to.

Setting up and utilizing teams that follow the Agile methodology is usually simple, making it easier for organizations to adopt Agile. However, it is important to remember that every Agile team is different from another. Therefore, a thorough understanding of Agile basics is important so that Agile principles and values that work for that particular team can be emphasized and improved while ironing out the weak areas.

More traditional project management methodologies, such as the Waterfall model, approach a project where the end product is developed as a single piece. Agile, on the other hand, takes a different approach by breaking down the development of the product into smaller increments. Therefore, Agile requires less initial planning and design while being easier to manage and deliver on time while staying within the budget.

For example, the Waterfall project management method will approach the building of a house from start to end with one deliverable and delivery date in mind. However, when it comes to Agile, the house's construction is broken down into smaller pieces, such as the foundation, walls, roof, interior, and exterior. Each of these increments will have predefined due dates.

Breaking a larger project into smaller, more manageable chunks is something that many individuals practice every day. For example, someone would rarely clean their entire home as a single project with an idea of a time or date to end the work in mind. Instead, many break it into smaller *increments*: kitchen, living room, bedrooms, and so on. This helps them manage the work better and get things done quickly without trying to clean the entire house in one go.

Increments that products are broken down into are called *iterations* or *sprints* in Agile. These iterations are *time-boxed*, which means that they have a fixed start and end date, where the team works on achieving the predefined targets for that particular increment. An increment can last from one week to four weeks, depending on the practices followed by the team or organization.

Every iteration is handled by a *cross-functional* team. A cross-functional team is one that attends to planning, design, analysis, development, and testing. Therefore, team members possessing skills that are required for covering all these areas need to be included in an

Agile team. For example, in a software development company, an Agile team should include business analysts, architects, developers, and quality assurance engineers.

The end of every iteration leaves a working product that can be brought to the stakeholders. This is one of the most important characteristics of Agile. A working version of the end product is maintained at the end of each iteration. Indeed, it may not have all the features of the end product; however, the stakeholders will be able to see the product being developed without having to wait until the end.

There are fewer risks associated with Agile project management because increments or working versions of the product are completed at the end of every iteration. Doing so enables the team to ensure that they are developing a product that meets client requirements and expectations.

Any mistakes or variations from requirements and expectations can be identified at the end of an iteration since the stakeholders can see a working version of the product. Fixing such issues is much less costly than identifying them at a later stage of product development or the very end.

For example, when a house is constructed using the Agile approach, the stakeholders will be able to see the foundation, walls, roof, etc., at the end of each increment. If there is anything that does not meet client requirements and expectations, it can be pointed out, and the team can fix those errors in the next iteration.

However, if the home is built using the Waterfall method, the client can only see a working version of the home at the end of construction. As such, if a certain characteristic of the roof does not agree with client requirements or expectations, the team will exceed the budget and time constraints and may need to redo some of the work on the interior and exterior while fixing the roof.

Agile methodology is also focused on enhancing communication among team members. It is prescribed that teams are accommodated close to each other in an office to communicate efficiently. This reduces the need for time-consuming communication methods such as calls, chats, and emails.

Every Agile team has a team member who represents that client. Stakeholders give consent to this particular team member to make decisions on their part when it comes to the work that is carried out by the team daily. The same person must also be available to answer any questions and provide clarifications whenever needed during iterations.

The end of an iteration provides a working version of the product or a product increment. The project team and stakeholders meet to review the product increment to ensure that the product that is being developed aligns with customer requirements and expectations. Agile is a project management methodology that can be used successfully in companies belonging to various sectors or industries. When properly implemented, it can bring teams toward highly satisfactory results.

2.1 What is The Manifesto?

Workers, companies, and clients became increasingly frustrated in the 1990s with existing project management methods such as the Waterfall. The end products were much different from the initial client requirements. Many projects were delayed while some were even canceled as clients were dissatisfied some of the companies' performances.

Most development teams were more concerned about documentation than developing products that met customer requirements and expectations. More importantly, traditional project management methodologies were unable to accommodate the changing demands of their customers well enough. Workers, specifically software developers, were also not as versatile.

There was a growing consensus in the software development industry that most companies were wasting resources by focusing on the less important things. The methods that were being used were not working for all projects, and a new methodology needed to be invented. An innovative and modern approach needed to be brought forth, so teams could be more independent and open to change, with higher productivity and efficiency.

As previously mentioned, seventeen individuals gathered at The Lodge in Snowbird. They went there to relax, eat, drink, ski, and, more importantly, find common ground. The result was the emergence of the Agile Manifesto for Software Development.

The document contained four core values and twelve principles that are prescribed for Agile software development. It was an alternative for project management methodologies largely driven by documentation and heavyweight processes that were proving to be unsuccessful for many types of projects.

This group, The Agile Alliance, published the *Agile Manifesto* that included the four values and twelve principles that they recommended for Agile software development. It must be noted that many Agile values and principles have been practiced by the experts belonging to the group for years. However, the manifesto made their vision more concrete that resulted in it taking the software development world by storm.

The team that worked on the *Agile Manifesto* included many experts and practitioners such as:

- Kent Back and Ron Jeffries, who co-created eXtreme Programming (XP)
- Andrew Hunt and Dave Thomas, who co-authored *The Pragmatic Programmer*
- Ken Schwaber and Jeff Sutherland, who co-created the Scrum framework
- Mike Beedle, co-author of *Agile Software Development with Scrum*
- Alistair Cockburn, the creator of Crystal Agile Methodology
- Jon Kern, who was a prominent lightweight process evangelist at the time

- Robert C Martin, also known as "Uncle Bob," a leading American software engineer and instructor
- Arie van Bennekum, the owner of Integrated Agile
- Martin Fowler, a partner at Thoughtworks
- Jim Highsmith, the creator of Adaptive Software Development (ASD)
- Brian Marick, an author and software testing expert
- Steve Mellor, inventor of Object-Oriented System Analysis (OOSA)
- Ward Cunningham, develop of the first Wiki
- James Grenning, author of Test-Driven Development

These men came up with the *Agile Manifesto* that would later change the way many companies manage projects.

2.2 Is Agile Only for Software Development?

It is fair to say that the majority of people aware of Agile project management have a background in the software development industry. Anyone who goes through the *Agile Manifesto* would clearly understand that the Agile methodology was intended for the software development practices. A look at the members of The Agile Alliance would also make it clear that the values and principles emerged in the software development world.

Agile may indeed have been created by a collective of software experts with the software development industry in mind. However, that does not limit Agile to the software industry because its values and principles can easily be applied to projects across a wide range of project types and industries.

Agile project management focuses on delivering value throughout the duration of a project instead of its very end. It is also highly open to change and better than many project management methodologies when it comes to responding to change. Agile also promotes creativity and innovation while maintaining the controlled development of products.

These are challenges that are present in not only software development but also in many other industries. Therefore, Agile can be used in numerous sectors and industries in addition to its popular use in software development.

2.3 Core Values and Principles of Agile

The Four Core Values of Agile

One of the main reasons for The Agile Alliance's gathering in 2001, and the *Agile Manifesto*, was to address many challenges that the software development industry was facing. Therefore, the four core values mentioned in the *Agile Manifesto* focus on what a team must do and avoid in an Agile environment. These four recommendations lay the foundation of how Agile teams function and how team members interact with each other and stakeholders.

Individuals and Interactions Over Processes and Tools

Agile methodology puts more value on people than tools and processes. The basic logic behind this value is that people and interactions involving people are easier to understand than tools and processes. It is a recognition of the optimal driving force of a development process, which is the human interactions instead of processes and tools.

When processes and tools drive the development of a product, the team becomes weaker when it comes to responding to change. As a result, they often fail to meet client requirements and expectations. However, when development is driven by individuals and their interactions, they can adapt to change better and, in return, are more likely to meet client requirements and expectations.

For example, processes and tools often unnecessarily complicate communication among individuals. However, when tools are taken out of the equation, and individuals are encouraged to communicate in person, communication becomes more effective and efficient. Agile also encourages communication whenever the need arises instead of following a process where communication is scheduled and limited to specific content. This contributes to teams being more responsive to change in Agile environments.

Working Software Over Comprehensive Documentation

There was an immense amount of documentation involved in the software development process when Agile was introduced to the world in 2001. Large amounts of time were dedicated to creating various documents, such as technical requirements, specifications, prospectus, user interfaced design documents, test and documentation plans, and approval documents. A substantial amount of documentation that existed in software development contributed to long delays in product development, with projects also exceeding budgets.

The *Agile Manifesto* emphasizes the delivery of working software instead of comprehensive documentation. Documentation is not entirely eliminated in Agile; however, it is streamlined so that those who contribute to the development of the product can work without being bogged down by documentation work.

Therefore, it must be highlighted that Agile does require some documentation, but it puts the main focus on delivering working versions of the product instead of documentation. For example, user stories are a type of document that enables developers to build new functionalities. Therefore, user stories are required in Agile.

Customer Collaboration Over Contract Negotiation

Before the inception of Agile project management, the project manager and customer would meet and negotiate when the product would be delivered and the details of the delivery. The requirements of the product are also negotiated in detail before any work is started. There would also be certain points in the project where they would meet and renegotiate according to the progress.

In project management methodologies such as Waterfall, the customer was involved in the process at the beginning and end. They were never involved during the time the product was being developed.

There was a need for customer collaboration during the development phase of the product, and it was addressed by the *Agile Manifesto*.

Agile recommended that project managers collaborate with clients instead of contract negotiation. The customer is involved throughout the development process, making it easier for project managers and developers to deliver an end product that meets customer requirements and expectations. Agile may dictate the intervals where customers can collaborate, but some projects may involve customers attending all meetings, especially when it comes to complex projects.

Responding to Change Over Following a Plan

The change was considered an expense in traditional project management, especially in software development. As a result, most traditional project management methodologies put much emphasis on the development of elaborate plans. A lot of time and resources were allocated to gather customer requirements and expectations and design features that would meet those needs.

The idea was to do as much planning as possible so that there would be less change. The approach may have looked good on paper but lacked practicality. Customer requirements and expectations were often misunderstood or wrongly captured, which required changes even after investing a significant amount of resources to avoid such occurrences. Some customer requirements and expectations would also change during the development process, which required changes.

Therefore, many project managers started to realize that change was inevitable in software development. That may have resulted in the *Agile Manifesto* being more focused on responding to change instead of strictly following a plan. Agile project management requires teams to respond to change instead of avoiding it. The approach helps teams quickly come up with solutions while developing a more useful and satisfactory product.

The 12 Principles of Agile

As mentioned, the *Agile Manifesto* described twelve principles for teams to follow in the implementation of Agile project management. These principles are focused on creating and nurturing a culture that is more welcoming to change, with the customer being more involved in the development process, especially compared to traditional project management approaches. The principles also focus on making product development more aligned with the needs of businesses.

1. Customer satisfaction by early and continuous delivery of valuable software.

Traditional project management methodologies only allow the customer to use and experience the product upon its completion. The product is usually checked and tested thoroughly before it is brought in front of the customer. This means that the customer is left in the dark regarding the product until it has been completed. The customer is not usually involved during the product development phase, making it difficult for the development team to introduce changes to the product even if they feel that they are necessary.

Keeping the customer involved throughout the development of the product, especially at an early stage, is one of the best ways to make them happy. Customers are given small increments of the product at the end of each sprint from an early stage in development. They can take a good look at the product and request changes if needed. The development team can make those changes to the product without those changes costing too many resources.

In traditional project management approaches, there is a large gap between documentation and the completion of the product, at which point the customer provides feedback. However, in Agile, this gap is made shorter, with the customer frequently providing feedback so that the end product is something that the customer actually wants instead of what the customer planned for at the start of the project.

2. Welcome changing requirements, even in late development.

There is a chance that a customer's requirements and expectations are wrongly interpreted by project managers. In traditional project management, such mistakes would only be identified at the end of the project, requiring a large amount of work to make the necessary changes. In Agile project management, most changes are likely to be requested by customers when they can be managed with minimal resources.

Agile reminds teams that change is inevitable. Therefore, teams are more welcoming towards changing requirements instead of dreading them. When a change is requested, the teams attend to the change in the next iteration itself without it causing more damage or requiring more time to fix later on.

A request for a change by a customer during the latter stages of development usually means that the development team will need to put in an extra effort and time to make that change. However, Agile recommends that teams welcome changes, even in late development, so that a great product is developed while satisfying the customer.

3. Deliver working software frequently (weeks rather than months).

This principle requires that the iterative process in the Agile approach consists of smaller time frames, ideally every few weeks instead of months. Such an iterative process not only improves the performance of teams but also involves the customer more frequently. A working increment of the product is delivered at the end of each stage, at which point the customer will review it. The shorter the time frame between iterations, the more efficient teams will be and with less space for drifting away from customer requirements.

This principle is often confused with the first principle, which states that teams should focus on releasing working products early. However, the third principle highlights the importance of smaller and more constant releases. When a release is small, there is less space for mistakes. For example, in the software scenario, a smaller release might not result in the discovery of many bugs, and the customer may not need any changes. Even the bugs and changes that are agreed upon can be quickly fixed in the next iteration while making progress with the product.

Regular releases provide the customer with regular opportunities to provide feedback regarding the product that is being developed. If a working product is released every week, the team ends up receiving feedback every week from the customer, which helps them stay on track. If a working product is only released every two months, there is a higher chance of bugs and variations from the customer's expectations due to the lack of feedback that was received.

4. Close, daily cooperation between business people and developers.

One of the biggest downfalls of traditional project management methodologies is that most stakeholders are unaware of the product that is being developed during the development stage of the project. Those who directly contribute to the project's development are usually kept away from business people, including customers. For example, in traditional software development methodologies, software developers hardly interact with business people. This results in teams casually going through the development stages without the customer seeing the product they are shaping.

However, Agile recommends that stakeholders are more involved, especially during the development stages, so that an end product with great value can be developed with frequent feedback. Barriers that stood between the developers and business people are recommended to be taken down, with interaction with each other every day—doing so results in improved transparency, understanding, and respect.

5. Projects are built around motivated individuals who should be trusted.

One of the main reasons for many traditional project management failures is the micromanagement of team members by project managers and others. Micromanaging team members often decreases morale and acts as a barrier against creativity and innovation. Projects that are built around team members who lack motivation often end with disappointments.

Agile addresses this issue by placing trust in team members instead of micromanaging them. There is a good reason why the particular team has been assembled. Therefore, they require trust. Placing trust in teams motivates them to work efficiently and effectively. The work is monitored, but team members are left alone as much as possible.

In such an environment, team members are confident. They often voice their opinions and share their knowledge with others that paves the way for creative and innovative solutions. A motivated individual is a better team player. Therefore, Agile environments lead to improved team performance.

6. A face-to-face conversation is the best form of communication (co-location).

Traditional project management methodologies focused a lot on the documentation of conversations, scheduling meetings, email streams, and collaborative tools. However, such methods often cost time, despite seeming to be making teams more efficient. The *Agile Manifesto* identified this obstacle, and the solution was to recognize face-to-face interactions as the best form of communication.

In a more traditional environment, a team member may be more focused on documenting a conversation or its outcome instead of understanding it. There may be time lost in between emails, memos, and interactions using collaborative tools. Valuable time to take action may be lost while team members wait for the next scheduled meeting. All this can be solved with simple face-to-face conversations.

Many organizations indeed have employees who work remotely. Under such scenarios, face-to-face conversations may not look like the most practical way for teams to communicate. However, tools such as Skype and Zoom enables teams to communicate face-to-face irrespective of where they are physically. Therefore, in the modern world, a team does not need to be in the same room to have a face-to-face conversation.

7. Working software is the primary measure of progress.

Before the inception of Agile, different factors were used to measure the progress of a project. However, most of these factors simply encouraged teams to complete *tasks* and move on to the next one. There was very little attention to the product that was being made or how usable it was. It led to end products that lacked quality and did not meet customer requirements and expectations. Therefore, analysis, models, and elaborate mock-ups have very little meaning when compared to a working product.

Agile prescribes that progress is measured based on the available working product instead of other factors, such as the number of tasks that have been completed. Thus, the progress of a project can be measured by how far the working product has evolved. Agile encourages teams to remain focused on what is more important: the working product. The working product is going to satisfy the customer.

8. Sustainable development, able to maintain a constant pace.

Working on complex and long projects often result in team members burning out after functioning at their best over a lengthy period. Many projects often start fast but lose pace as they move further into the development phase. Therefore, sustaining a constant development pace was one of the main areas that Agile wished to address.

The eighth principle in the *Agile Manifesto* dictates that the development speed needs to be sustainable throughout the course of the project. Therefore, teams are recommended not to undertake any more work than they can sustain over a long period. Working hard is encouraged, but overworking themselves is discouraged altogether.

The repeatable iterative pattern in Agile helps teams establish a healthy development pace where they are efficient without overtaxing themselves with too much work. An iteration should not have less or more work than any other; every iteration should involve just the right amount of work. Maintaining such a consistent and sustainable development speed keeps team members free of stress while the project progresses at an acceptable pace.

9. Continuous attention to technical excellence and good design.

It is natural for most businesses to consider lengthy production times as a cost. The longer a product takes to build, the longer a company needs to wait to be paid and start building the next product. Furthermore, many businesses believe that the end-user does not really care about their technical excellence. Technical excellence, in most cases, does not generate a direct income for a company. However, that does not mean companies should focus less on it.

If drawing a good technical design for a product is neglected, it might affect the product speed. Without a good design, a product will be difficult to make and hence take more time. Furthermore, products with poor designs are usually more difficult or even impossible to change concerning changing customer requirements and expectations.

When it comes to small projects, it might make sense to develop the product instead of spending a lot of time designing it. However, complex projects require teams to focus on technical quality and great design. Great design does not need to be created before the development of the product begins. The design can evolve as the product is developed. However, teams need to be provided with the time and resources to do so.

Agile nurtures good designs and technical excellence by encouraging teams to improve their work after every iteration. Anything that needs to be fixed must be fixed now without having to come back later. The team is also expected to learn from mistakes and improve so that the same mistakes are not repeated, costing valuable resources. Focusing on great designs and technical quality adds immense value to a product. Customers will take notice, and the business will soon start benefiting since satisfied customers often help companies.

10. Simplicity—the art of maximizing the amount of work not done—is essential.

It is safe to say that Agile is a project management methodology that is more focused on getting work done and adding more value to products instead of formalities. Many procedures followed traditionally in companies may no longer be relevant in an Agile environment. Teams might opt to ignore certain procedures, automate time-consuming manual tasks, and use existing libraries instead of writing their own.

Doing all this gives teams more time to focus on the work that needs to be done and add more value to the product they are developing. The aim is to move as quickly as possible by eliminating unnecessary complexities. Teams are encouraged to keep things as simple as possible. Simplicity has proven to be a great ingredient when it comes to streamlining processes. In any iteration, tasks that need to be completed are the main focus of every team member. Documenting, planning, and adding extra features are not considered as priorities until the work that needs to be done is completed.

11. Best architectures, requirements, and designs emerge from self-organizing teams.

This principle is aimed at making some of the earlier principles realistic in working environments. How Agile recommends that developers and businesses communicate directly and regularly and why working software is more important than theoretical models was discussed earlier. How motivated individuals contribute to producing high-quality products was also established above. By comparison, this states that, for all this to succeed, teams must be allowed to self-organize themselves without too much control from above.

In an Agile environment, teams are given the power to organize everything related to product development. They decide when they want to communicate, how the tasks are completed, how the work is going to be divided among team members, and more. Such an environment is considered to enhance productivity and quality since those who directly develop the product start to take more ownership.

There is a big difference between being held responsible and taking ownership of a product that is being developed. When an individual is being held responsible for a certain task, there is a sense of obligation and stress around it. However, taking ownership of the work that someone does comes from within themselves. It is a choice instead of something that's assigned by a superior. As a result, teams tend to be more efficient and effective when left to function independently.

12. Regularly, the team reflects on how to become more effective and adjusts accordingly.

Agile project management methodology recommends that teams take the time to regularly look at themselves and the work they have been doing so that they can make collective and individual improvements and adjustments to be more effective in the future. Expecting a self-organizing team to be perfect is unrealistic, no matter how well qualified the team members. Therefore, teams must be encouraged to reflect on themselves and identify areas that they can improve on.

In Agile environments, teams usually complete a product increment during an iteration and pause. Then, they will take a bit of time to reflect on the previous iteration. During these sessions, team members will identify areas that they can improve on, both as a team and as individuals. Then they will proceed to the next iteration.

Therefore, Agile methodology reduces complacency in teams. Being complacent is one of the biggest mistakes an individual, team, or company can make in any business, be it software development or manufacturing. Agile reduces complacency by requiring teams to continuously and regularly improve themselves by reflecting on their most recent work.

Project managers often promote sessions where teams evaluate their work and performance and discuss ways to improve. Doing so benefits companies since teams become more productive while also evolving, with individuals gaining more skills. Furthermore, products also increase in value as mistakes are avoided throughout the development as teams become more capable.

2.4 What Does an Agile Team Look Like?

A small group of individuals assigned to the same effort or project is considered a *team* in an Agile environment. Most individuals who belong to Agile teams are usually full-time employees. However, part-time specialists may join an Agile team and contribute to the project if the need arises.

The idea of a team brings shared accountability to that group of people. It does not matter if the outcomes of their efforts are good or bad; the entire team is attributed to them instead of narrowing things down to any member of the team. It is recommended that an Agile team possesses all the required skills and expertise that are required to develop a product.

For example, a team that is developing software must include programmers, architects, and testers, as well as individuals with business and domain knowledge, such as business analysts. Results are given more weight in Agile development instead of roles and responsibilities.

Therefore, a software programmer may complete certain tasks traditionally considered someone else's responsibility, such as requirement and performance analysis and testing. The focus is on getting the work done instead of limiting team members to specific roles and responsibilities.

One of the most common errors that many companies make when implementing Agile is mistaking a *team* as a *group*. A group of people working together may not always be an Agile team. Furthermore, a group member may contribute to multiple projects simultaneously without considering them to be in more than one *team*. A group of people may also be any number above three.

In an Agile environment, a team should have a minimum of three members and ideally, a maximum of ten members. Agile teams are usually co-located—or they function at their best when they are co-located. Members of an Agile team are dedicated to a single project on a full-time basis. They should not be spread across more than one project at the same time.

Agile teams are cross-functional, which means that they can function on their own without depending on individuals who do not belong to the team. That is why an Agile team should possess all the skills and expertise to complete the tasks that it is assigned. Agile teams usually have a limited number of team roles according to the Agile framework that is being used.

For example, Scrum is an Agile framework, and an Agile team using the Scrum framework needs to have individuals filling the roles of Scrum Master, Product Owner, and Team Members.

Collaboration with Customers

Agile teams regularly and continuously interact with the customer. The methodology states that the development team must provide a working version of the product as early as possible. This is usually available at the end of the first iteration, where the customer can review the product increment and provide feedback. Any changes that are needed are also identified and requested, reducing the need for costly changes.

The customer interacts with an Agile team throughout the development phase. They communicate swiftly, and the customer's requirements and expectations are easily understood by the team compared to solely referring to documents. Face-to-face interaction with the team also helps customers explain their requirements clearly without being misunderstood. Even if they are misunderstood, the mistakes can be corrected at the end of the next iteration.

Compared to traditional project management methodologies, such as Waterfall, Agile is preferred by customers as they communicate directly with the development team instead of someone who represents them. Information is unlikely to be misinterpreted as a result. Regular and continuous interactions between Agile teams and customers also pave the way for developing high-quality products with great value.

Daily Communication

There is a big difference between a group of people who work together and a *team*. A team is a cohesive unit that efficiently communicates and collaborates to achieve a set of goals. The quality of teamwork is determined by six key components: coordination, communication, balanced contributions, support, cohesion, and effort. Teamwork quality directly impacts a team's performance and the success of the project.

Agile methodology believes that teams are more successful when members of those teams rely on each other instead of various tools and processes. Working together as a team gives team members the power and boldness to come up with innovative solutions instead of following traditional methods. Therefore, teamwork is one of the most important ingredients of Agile methodology.

Agile teams plan and organize their work among themselves by quick daily meetings. They are also encouraged to have face-to-face conversations whenever needed instead of waiting for the next scheduled meeting or relying on other mediums, such as chats, emails, and collaborative tools. Team members are located in the same area close to each other to facilitate face-to-face conversations. The team often invites stakeholders for brainstorming meetings who might help them with valuable inputs.

The entire Agile team connects at daily meetings to become aware of their progress and any issues. These face-to-face encounters are quick and to the point. At times, problems that certain team members are facing may be brought up with the entire team collaboratively making plans to overcome those obstacles. Such collaboration and trust build teamwork while positively contributing to the progress of the project. The focus of daily communication also makes Agile more sustainable.

Motivated Individuals

Motivation is one of the most important ingredients in maintaining productivity and performance throughout the development phase of a project. It becomes more important as the size, complexity, and the duration of the project increases. Motivation drives teams toward putting in their best effort every day for an extended length of time without burning out.

Agile environments aim to give individuals plenty of motivation to work toward the goals of their teams collaboratively. They are passionate about the work they do. They also do their work while supporting their team members, as achieving the goals of an individual is not considered a success in an Agile setting. Fueled by motivation, support, trust, and consistency, Agile teams often establish highly productive rhythms sustained throughout projects resulting in highly satisfactory outcomes.

Creating an environment to nurture motivated team members is not easy, especially if a team is new to Agile. Most companies start with changing their floor plans to open offices. Teams can perform efficiently in such settings as their team members are just a few steps away whenever they need to have a quick conversation. Such a floor plan also encourages team members to collaborate more and enhance brainstorming among teams while keeping individuals focused on team activities.

It is important to realize that Agile teams achieve progress through individual work. Therefore, individual workspaces also need to be available for team members. They provide a quieter area, which can be used to perform individual work toward the team goal.

Self-Organizing Teams

Teams are trusted to organize how they will complete the work they wish to achieve during an iteration in Agile. They decide how the work is going to be executed and who is going to do which tasks. There is no involvement from the management regarding assigning tasks to team members or tracking tasks assigned to individuals. An Agile team is completely trusted by the management to make the right decisions.

It is an arrangement that everyone involved needs to appreciate. Managers can stop pushing people to do their work. Workers can stop managers from looking over their shoulders all the time. The arrangement needs team members to be very confident about their work. They must also be prepared to overcome obstacles that might arise. However, they can take comfort in knowing that their team members will be there to support them.

Accountability and responsibility are shared equally among all team members of an Agile team. As a result, they are required to perform both as individuals and in team roles. Each member needs to complete the work that is assigned to them by the team. Furthermore, they must be willing to step outside of their individual roles to overcome obstacles as a team whenever one or more team members are faced with difficulty.

When a team fails to meet the expected goals during an iteration, they identify the mistakes and learn. There is no direction from the management. Improvement is organically created within the team and, commonly, newly formed Agile teams have an Agile mentor.

It takes teams some time to become self-organizing without running into problems. Coaching and training need to be provided so that teams learn about how Agile works and improves as the project moves on. Even a team that is functioning very well may benefit from the existence of an Agile mentor as it enables team members to improve.

Agile teams are also given the freedom to determine what tools and processes they are going to follow. The tools and processes they choose may differ from those used by other teams in the same company. The company can provide the tools; however, the team is not entitled to request training on how to use the tools and processes that they choose to work with.

Continuous Improvements as Teams

Agile teams need to regularly and routinely reflect on their performance so they can improve. As a result, Agile teams are dedicated to continuous improvement. Naturally, Agile teams do not respond well to commands and orders. However, they are more open to coaching and mentoring. Retrospectives are sessions that are scheduled routinely after the completion of an iteration to facilitate team improvement.

During such sessions, team members talk about the things that went both well and wrong. They then collectively identify ways to improve the process while avoiding mistakes, so the next iteration runs smoothly. Great Agile teams use retrospectives to their advantage, as continuous improvements not only make their lives easier but also improve their skills and benefit their organization.

It may take Agile teams some time to gauge their optimal performance levels while keeping sustainability in mind. Newly formed teams are prescribed to go slow in the beginning and gradually increase the amount of work they take on during every iteration. Furthermore, these increments to the workload need to stop when they feel their maximum capacity is met. Continuous improvement does not mean that teams need to take on a larger workload.

Instead, teams are encouraged to understand the most work they can do while sustaining productivity. Many teams that undertake larger workloads experience burnouts, where team members are overworked and too stressed. Therefore, the workload that an Agile team undertakes needs to be such that the same level of productivity can be maintained for a long time—at least until the project is completed. Furthermore, teams need to keep a buffer for unplanned work and unexpected events that might come their way.

2.5 Agile Team Roles

Agile is a project management methodology introduced to solve many problems companies and clients face using traditional project management methods. The approach is focused on breaking goals down into smaller, independent products that can be incrementally developed and released. The Agile workflow requires highly coordinated teams to keep up with demanding schedules and short task spans. As a result, Agile team roles need to be well defined and understood by every team member.

Team Lead (Team Coach or Project Lead)

This individual is responsible for providing an Agile team with coaching and guidance. The team leader also needs to obtain the resources the team needs and remove any factors that harm the team and its performance. The role of the team leader does not involve much planning as the entire team works on planning.

Many wrongly think that a team lead is the manager of an Agile team; however, the role does not reflect a rank. It instead reflects responsibility and knowledge that are used to guide an Agile team in the right direction.

The Product Owner

An individual who has a good sense and vision about the end product being developed is usually trusted with the Product Owner role. He or she is often a key stakeholder or an executive in a company. The Product Owner must guide a team through the development process while correcting mistakes and initiating changes whenever required.

In an Agile environment, the Product Owner is considered to have a role similar to the captain of a ship. The captain directs the ship on the correct path while establishing order among the ship's crew. The captain also has the final word on any changes that need to be made aboard the ship.

The Product Owner provides a team with similar guidance and direction by carrying out a range of duties. One of the most important responsibilities of a Product Owner is to define the work that must be done. The Product Owner makes project objectives clear and transparent to a team while setting standards in terms of the work quality that needs to be delivered.

The work that the team completes shapes the end product. However, the Product Owner is responsible for creating tasks that will take the team there. A Product Owner is usually an individual who is passionate about the product and has a clear idea and vision about why the product needs to exist. Such an individual will instantly know when the product is not being shaped right.

Product Owners need to be very good at communicating with the team as a collective and with individual team members. They must maintain clarity and transparency at high levels so that the entire team is on the same page regarding the product they are developing. Therefore, the Product Owner participates in daily stand-up meetings of an Agile team and can also call any one-on-one ad hoc meetings if they feel it necessary.

The Product Owner is responsible for ensuring that the work done by the team is flowing smoothly. Furthermore, the Product Owner must ensure that the end product is in its most valuable form. They must also understand the priority of tasks that need to be completed based on project circumstances as well as feedback from stakeholders.

The Product Owner also must ensure that the team can deliver project iterations continuously with precise cycle planning. The end goal of a Product Owner is to make sure that the development process brings value for customers and other stakeholders to develop a product of value. The Product Owner is required to maintain communications with the development team, end-users, partners, and business executives throughout the project.

The Team Member

Workers with diverse expertise are known as team members. They directly contribute to the development of a product. Front-end and back-end software developers, designers, copywriters, architects, and videographers can all be members of a team in a particular sector where their expertise is used to develop a product. Team members may have different skills, but they are all responsible for getting the work done.

The majority of an Agile team is made up of team members. If the Product Owner is the ship's captain, the team members are the crew. It is natural for team members to bring a variety of skills, expertise, and traits to an Agile team. Individuals who are creative and can work autonomously usually thrive in Agile environments.

A team member is considered a *specialist* who contributes to the development of the product. Team members must work both collaboratively and independently. They can consult each other for brainstorming or meet with the Product Owner to find answers to any questions they might have. They must also work efficiently while avoiding distractions.

In Agile, team members are given a lot of freedom to direct and organize themselves and their work. Therefore, it is safe to say that most individuals feel empowered in an Agile environment, leading them to take ownership of their work. This usually results in individuals performing much better compared to traditional project management styles. Agile also encourages teams to improve continuously, and some of the positive effects also contribute to the personal development of team members.

Stakeholders

It is true that the stakeholder does not directly contribute to the development of the product, and are not always involved. However, stakeholders play an important role when it comes to shaping the end product that is being developed by an Agile team. A stakeholder can be a business executive, end-user, investor, production support staff member, external auditor, or a team member from another team.

Stakeholders are usually picked depending on the inputs they can provide or are required for the smooth functioning of an Agile team. The inputs also often affect the project direction. Successful stakeholders can help Agile teams develop products that meet business goals and end-users' expectations. Furthermore, stakeholders can, at times, address certain challenges that are experienced by team members.

Representatives from legal departments, customers, technical experts, account managers, marketing experts, salespeople, and many other professionals can be considered stakeholders of a project depending on its nature and the nature of the product. Stakeholders provide valuable insights regarding the end product and the way it is meant to be used. It is common for stakeholders to work collaboratively with Product Owners during an iteration and provide feedback when the released product increment is reviewed.

Agile Mentor

Individuals who act as coaches and mentors for teams that are new to Agile are known as Agile Mentors. Therefore, an Agile Mentor must have a vast amount of experience with Agile projects. They must also share their knowledge with an Agile team by providing coaching and mentoring instead of giving out orders and commands.

Mentors are instrumental in helping new project teams understand how Agile works and achieve high-performance levels. The Agile Mentor is merely there to provide guidance and direction to an Agile team. He or she will not contribute to the development process. Thus, the role of an Agile Mentor is an optional one.

Additional Agile Roles for Larger Projects

The roles that were described above are common in Agile teams. However, some companies may include more Agile roles, especially when working on larger and more complex projects. A good example is the inclusion of domain and technical experts to ensure that the development team does not experience any gaps in knowledge and expertise in terms of domain and technology.

It is also common for testing and audit teams to join Agile teams. These teams work with the Agile team throughout the development process to provide them assistance with testing and auditing. Independent testing teams are useful when testing complex products where there is a high chance of coming across mistakes that testers in the Agile team may miss. Therefore, the presence of such individuals aids in the product development process.

When it comes to a project that involves multiple sub-systems that are handled by separate independent Agile teams, an Integrator is brought in so that sub-systems are integrated properly and to a sound plan. The Integrator ensures that sub-systems are tested properly and might even bring in external testing teams if the need arises.

Some complex projects may require an experienced architect. An Architect Owner is included in Agile teams for such projects where the Architect Owner makes plans and takes care of decision-making. The roles of Architect Owner and Integrator may exist in the same project if it involves complex, multiple sub-systems.

2.6 What Is the Overall Goal of Agile?

Agile is a modern approach to project management that intends to: make project management simpler, avoid long delays, and ensure that products are not different from customer requirements and expectations. It is a flexible approach that allows projects to be broken down into smaller and easily manageable tasks. These tasks are included in short iterations that have specific start and end dates. The development team focuses on completing the tasks within the iteration.

At the end of every iteration, a working or usable version of the product is brought forward to the customer. This enables the customer to see and use working versions of the product regularly, especially starting from a very early stage in development. As a result, the client is in regular agreement about the product that is being built. Any changes that are required are added to the next iteration.

The Agile method allows teams to organize themselves and deliver work fast. They can also quickly respond to change. Teams can quickly re-evaluate the current circumstances and adjust the work they are going to do in an increment instead of trying to keep to a plan during the entire product development phase. Agile methodology teaches teams to embrace change instead of avoiding it. As a result, Agile methodology has been highly successful in projects with changing requirements.

Agile may look like a complex methodology to anyone new to it. It might also seem difficult to manage. On the contrary, Agile is one of the most straightforward methodologies out there that make managing teams much easier.

Another goal of Agile is to create an environment where creativity is encouraged. Some projects may begin without the end product clearly defined. Such projects need teams that can quickly adapt to change and come up with creative solutions and ideas. The Agile approach is highly suited for such projects that involve high levels of change, creativity, and innovation.

The Agile approach was originally intended for software development. However, it has been successfully adopted by companies in different sectors since the Agile values and principles can be applied to any industry. As a result, it is common to see the Agile methodology in motion in education, marketing, military, construction, and automotive industries.

Agile intends to create shorter development cycles instead of being limited to a single or too few cycles during the product development phase. As a result, Agile provides frequent releases. These shorter cycles help teams to respond to any changes requested by the client easily. Agile project management involves a basic process that includes a range of activities, such as project planning, the creation of the product roadmap, planning of releases and iterations, daily stand-up meetings, reviews, and retrospectives.

Project Planning

A project needs to begin with a clear plan. Although Agile involves less planning than traditional project management approaches, it still requires a certain level of planning. Project planning in Agile includes understanding the project's end goal, the project's value to the client, and how the end goal is going to be achieved.

Some individuals also develop a project scope; however, it is important to remember that project scope is subject to change since the purpose of Agile is to embrace change. Therefore, the likelihood of features being added or removed from a project scope is high in Agile.

Product Roadmap Creation

This activity breaks the end product into a set of features. These features must create the end product once combined since the team will develop each of those features during iterations. Therefore, if the end product is not broken down into the correct features, the team may face difficulties towards the end of the project while posing the risk of delays.

The Product Backlog is also developed at this point. The Product Backlog lists all the features that should be in the final product according to customer requirements and expectations. Teams use the Product Backlog to choose tasks that they are going to complete in a particular iteration. Therefore, the Product Backlog must be complete so that any tasks or features are not missed.

Release Planning

Traditional project management methodologies such as the Waterfall method only involve one release, provided on the implementation date. Agile, on the other hand, involves many short development cycles. As a result, features of the end product are released at the end of every cycle. Creating a plan for these releases is advised. Release plans may change while the project runs its course. Therefore, it is recommended that the release plan is revisited before the start of every iteration or development cycle.

Iteration Planning

Agile teams usually plan what will be done during an iteration by choosing tasks from the Product Backlog. The team then decides which team member will contribute to each task while ensuring that tasks are distributed evenly between the entire team. Teams are encouraged to visually track the workflow, using whiteboards and similar methods, to maintain transparency and understanding among the team. The visual representation of tasks also helps teams identify and eliminate bottlenecks.

Daily Meetings

The Agile methodology prescribes daily meetings where the team gets together and assesses the work that has been completed and the work that remains in the current iteration. They then collectively make plans for the day while ensuring that they are on track to complete all the tasks in the iteration on time.

It is recommended that daily meetings are only limited to fifteen minutes. Furthermore, they should not serve the purpose of brainstorming or problem-solving. Their purpose is to simply review the tasks at hand and determine what the team will achieve within the day. Agile environments encourage daily stand-up meetings since sitting down usually causes meetings to drag.

Reviews and Retrospectives

Agile is a project management methodology that is intended to reduce the chances of the end product varying from the original customer requirements and expectations. This is achieved with the customer being provided working increments of the product throughout the development phase. Every cycle or iteration that is completed provides the customer with a working version of the product that they can review.

Therefore, the customer is aware of the product that is being developed from an early stage of the development process and can identify any changes that need to be made. Such changes are easier and less costly to make compared to identifying changes at the end of development. Therefore, reviews are a key part of Agile development.

The Agile methodology also encourages teams to seek ways to continue regularly. As a result, retrospectives are held at the end of each iteration. During a retrospective, team members reflect on what went right and wrong during the iteration. They then discuss how they are going to improve as a team during the next iteration.

2.7 How Is Agile Different Than Other Methodologies

The Agile project management methodology was introduced to solve many of the challenges experienced in software development with traditional project management methods. As a result, Agile introduced a novel approach compared to many of those traditional project management methodologies, with several differences between them.

Concurrent Development and Testing

Agile breaks down the end product into smaller increments. The team then works on developing each of these product increments during iterations that last for a fixed amount of time. During an iteration, development and testing happen at the same time. Concurrent development and testing allow better communication among developers, testers, managers, and customers.

This was a major difference that Agile introduced compared to traditional methods, such as the Waterfall Model or Linear Sequential Life Cycle Model. The Waterfall Model follows a sequential order where the development team moves on to a stage upon the completion of the other. As a result, testing begins upon the completion of the previous step, which usually is development. Therefore, development and testing do not happen concurrently in the Waterfall method.

Stages are Repeated in Cycles

Agile breaks down the product development phase into cycles or iterations. Key parts of product development, including planning, development, and testing, are involved in every cycle. Once a cycle is completed, the team moves on to the next cycle, where key steps, including planning, development, and testing, occur again.

Methods such as Waterfall, on the other hand, are strictly sequential. It involves eight stages where the completion of one stage enables the team to move on to the next. However, once the team moves on to a certain stage upon the completion of another, they cannot go back. Therefore, if a change is discovered towards the end of the process, their model does not define a way to facilitate it.

The Waterfall method originated and became highly popular in the construction and manufacturing sectors. Processes in these industries are structured where changes are usually rare and unfeasible. Therefore, changes are not accommodated in such industries. The Waterfall method is suitable for such processes where there is a low chance of change. Such processes also allow for detailed documentation that the Waterfall method requires.

Prior Experience and Knowledge

The use of traditional project management methods does not require team members to have prior knowledge. Methods such as Waterfall are very easy to follow even for an individual who has not been part of a Waterfall project before. In most cases, the Waterfall method can be used with the presence of an experienced project manager.

Agile, on the other hand, requires prior knowledge. Team members, customers, and company leaders need to know how Agile works and things they should and should not do in an Agile environment. The difference between the way things are done in a traditional environment and an Agile environment also contributes to this need for Agile knowledge.

Individuals who play roles, such as team leads, product owners, team members, and stakeholders, all need to understand their roles clearly. They must also be aware of Agile values and principles for the methodology to be successful. As a result, most companies that are new to Agile introduce Agile Mentors to their teams so the team members can be guided and directed in the right direction.

Enforcing Discipline vs. Trust and Freedom

Project management methodologies such as the Waterfall method are strict about how things and done and when they are done. Discipline is enforced with strict guidelines on focusing on requirements, comprehensive documentation, and following the sequence of phases strictly irrespective of the project and customer needs. Although the method is a well-documented approach that enables stakeholders and customers to understand the product, it may not be practical in many instances.

For example, if a team misses an important feature of the project during development, which is only discovered at the testing phase, there is no way for the team to go back and develop that feature. However, it may play a key role in the product. Enforcing discipline fails in such instances.

Agile, on the other hand, gives teams the freedom to get things done so that a great product is created. In what sequence activities take place does not concern Agile. Agile teams are trusted by the management to function independently and make the right decisions to complete a product full of value.

Avoiding Change vs. Embracing Change

The way that traditional project management methods approach change is their drawback and the reason behind the invention of the

Agile methodology. Most traditional methods try to avoid change through extensive analysis, planning, and documentation. This is because most such methodologies are linear or sequential. The teams cannot switch between phases. Therefore, there is no space to accommodate changes in such methods.

Agile, on the other hand, takes an approach where change is embraced. The approach consists of smaller and regular development cycles that produce usable iterations of the product that the project is gradually building. The testers can test and find bugs and mistakes before the end of the iteration, while the customer also gets the chance to see the product increment and provide feedback. Such interactions sometimes result in changes being made to the product. However, Agile teams have a mindset where such changes are welcomed since they increase the end product's value.

The Delivery of Working Software

Most traditional project management methodologies do not deliver a working product until the end of the project. As a result, customers only get the chance to see the product once it has been completed. Such an approach may only work where the customer exactly knows the product they need. However, this is not the case most of the time, and that was one reason that inspired the introduction of the *Agile Manifesto.*

Most traditional project management methodologies are focused on gathering customer requirements and analyzing them at the beginning of the project. Then these requirements are comprehensively documented. The development of the product does not begin until all these stages are complete. Then the customer needs to wait a long time until the end of the project to see a working product.

However, most traditional methods do not account for the fact that the customer requirements and expectations can change during the project. Therefore, they may not see much value in the product they needed at the start of the project. Therefore, traditional project management methods do not accommodate or suit projects where there is a high chance of changing requirements.

Agile, on the other hand, is focused on developing working increments of the product regularly. More importantly, the development begins early with the client being able to see releases from an early stage of the project without waiting until the end. As a result, any changes that the customer wishes to be made can be easily completed in the next iteration. The delivery of working versions at regular intervals makes Agile a great methodology to develop products with ever-changing requirements or if a customer is not certain about the product they need.

Team Characteristics

There are significant differences between teams in traditional project management methodologies and Agile. Important attributes are the definition of a team, the way teams operate, team leadership, the types of experts that belong to a team, and many others.

Agile teams have very little structure, while most other teams are structured with permanent team members and roles. Agile team members are interchangeable. As a result, the work is completed faster. The self-organizing quality of Agile teams eliminates the need for project managers in Agile environments. However, most other project management methodologies require the guidance and management expertise of project managers.

Agile teams do not feature team members with different ranks. Every member of the team is treated with the same level of respect, and the work is evenly distributed among all team members. Other management methods feature teams where ranks are involved, and micromanagement of teams is present.

An Agile team consists of all kinds of experts that are needed to develop a product without relying on anyone outside of the team. However, other project methodologies may instead focus on creating teams based on expertise. Such teams are provided targets to achieve by their superiors. However, Agile teams organize themselves; they select the workload that they are going to achieve in an iteration.

Most traditional project management approaches do not involve or require high levels of team coordination. However, Agile requires teams to coordinate to the best of their abilities so that goals can be met collaboratively. Team members are encouraged to support each other as they pull their weight in an Agile environment.

Funding and Risk

Traditional project management methodologies are usually considered safe to manage fixed-price projects. Risk agreements are signed at the beginning of such projects that result in reduced risks. However, when Agile is used for fixed-price projects, it may become stressful for the company, especially if continuous changes delay the project or if the project's completion takes longer than the company estimated. The Agile methodology works best with projects that have non-fixed funding. The client agrees to pay the company for its resources, even if estimated delivery dates need to be extended since the focus is on developing a product full of value.

Requirements and Changes

When it comes to more traditional project management methods, requirements are gathered, analyzed, and agreed upon at the beginning of the project. This phase is usually completed and thoroughly documented before the development of the product. The developers then refer to documented requirements and develop the product. Upon the completion of the development, the testing begins. The developers then fix any bugs detected by the testers, and the product is delivered to the client.

If there is a misunderstanding during the initial requirements gathering stage about a requirement, the client only gets to find out at the end of the project. This may happen due to confusion. The client may also change his or her mind about a certain requirement while the product is in development. Some changes in the business environment might also make certain features of the product less effective. However, traditional project management approaches do not consider such scenarios due to their linear approach to product development.

Agile, on the other hand, requires the Product Owner to regularly prepare requirements upon receiving feedback from the customer at the end of every iteration. Neither the development team nor the customer completely relies on the requirements gathered before starting the project. Requirements and changes are established as the product is developed incrementally.

There are numerous advantages that this approach offers both the development team and the customer. The product that is being developed offers more value to the customer. As a result, the customer is likely to be more satisfied with the project. Any lapses in requirement analysis can be quickly accounted for without costing the company much, since the customer is more involved in the development process, increasing the chances of correcting such mistakes.

Chapter 3: Scrum Project Management

The Agile methodology emerged as a result of the failures of prominent and popular project management methodologies. The linear and sequential nature of those methodologies and the focus on documentation were seen as disadvantages, especially when it came to complex projects with high probabilities of change.

The Agile Alliance introduced the *Agile Manifesto* that declared four values and twelve principles that aimed to change the way projects were managed in the software development industry.

Most of the values and principles were different from what was mentioned in the Project Management Body of Knowledge (PMBOK). There was a greater emphasis on communication, teamwork, collaboration, team independence, the delivery of functioning software in increments, and the ability to adapt to change. The Agile approach was also one of the earliest methodologies to embrace change as it was a reality in business; however, most traditional methods considered change to be costly.

Scrum is an Agile framework that enables teams to efficiently and effectively work on projects in unison. The framework takes many Agile values and principles a step further, enabling teams to function at their best. Scrum framework describes specific meetings, tools, and roles that can be used to help teams organize and manage their work efficiently and productively.

Important team traits, such as learning from experience, working on a problem independently, and reflecting on wins and losses in search of improvement, are highlighted in Scrum. While the Scrum framework initially gained immense popularity in software development, it soon proved to apply to all kinds of teams across sectors and industries with great success. As a result, the framework became very popular.

Although Scrum is merely an Agile framework, it is often mistaken as a project management methodology. Furthermore, many individuals wrongly think that Scrum and Agile are the same approaches. Certain Agile values and principles have indeed been inspired by Scrum. For example, Scrum's focus on continuous improvement through regular team reflecting on wins and losses is one of the principles described in the *Agile Manifesto*.

However, Scrum and Agile are not the same approach or methodology. While Agile methodology is more of a mindset, Scrum is merely a framework that can use that mindset to get work done. Teams often struggle to get into the Agile mindset as it is very different from traditional project management approaches. The Scrum framework is a great way for teams to start practicing Agile principles and develop valuable products without confusion.

One of the greatest attributes of the Scrum framework is that it is easy for teams to adopt. The framework is based on gradual learning and adjusting to changing factors. Scrum assumes that a team is not experienced in the Agile way of thinking at the beginning of a project. It accommodates step-by-step learning for teams making it easy to adapt.

Furthermore, the Scrum framework is structured so that it enables teams to adjust to changing business environs and user requirements naturally. Re-prioritization is built into the Scrum process along with short cycles making it easier for teams to learn and improve in such business climates and projects.

Although structures, Scrum isn't too rigid, which is one of the key reasons behind its popularity. The Scrum framework can be tailored to the needs of a team, project, or company. Numerous successful Scrum theories exist when it comes to how teams can successfully adapt the Scrum framework, and any suitable combination of theories can be used as needed.

3.1 Scrum vs. Agile

Many individuals and even companies are confused when it comes to the relationship between Agile and Scrum. Some think that Scrum is a methodology just like Agile. Some believe that they are the same. While Agile and Scrum may be similar in many ways, they are not the same.

To put in the simplest terms, Agile is a methodology. The *Agile Manifesto* explains four core values and twelve guiding principles that can be used to help teams approach software development or the development of any other product differently to the sequential approach. Therefore, what the *Agile Manifesto* describes is a methodology and mindset or team.

When a team successfully adopts the values and principles of Agile, they can work productively and collaboratively to develop the product in small increments while increasing the product's value and dealing with changes through regular interactions with the customer. Agile simply provides guidelines on the mindset that can take teams there. However, Agile does not provide steps to achieve its values and principles.

Scrum, on the other hand, is a framework that helps teams adopt the Agile way of thinking and doing things. Scrum provides simple steps, which teams that do not have much or any prior Agile experience can follow to get into the Agile mindset. Therefore, teams use the Scrum framework to follow the Agile methodology.

Decision-making in Scrum is based on real-world outcomes instead of assumptions or speculations. Therefore, decisions can be easily justified, and they often tend to be the correct ones. Furthermore, there is very little disagreement or debate among team members regarding most decisions since they are based on real-world results.

Agile emphasizes the delivery of working increments of the product. Therefore, the development phase needs to be broken down into smaller cycles. However, there is no clear guideline about the exact or ideal duration of an iteration in the *Agile Manifesto.* However, in Scrum, the development phase is divided into short cycles known as sprints, which usually last for one or two weeks.

There is also very little uncertainty in the Scrum framework. All the defined roles, responsibilities, and meetings remain constant in Scrum. Therefore, Scrum enables teams to focus their energy and focus on the necessary unpredictability while reducing the unnecessary.

Going Agile as a team is difficult. It requires every team member to adopt and be in agreement about its values and principles. However, Scrum is a framework that incorporates Agile values and principles into a team so that it starts thinking and practicing the teachings of the *Agile Manifesto.*

Everyday communication. Short development cycles. Value to working product. Regular releases. Receiving regular feedback and embracing change. Continuous improvements through regularly reflecting on team performance. The framework makes Agile achievable for teams.

3.2 Scrum Roles

Scrum framework focuses on developing products incrementally with the use of small, self-organizing teams. A Scrum team should have more than three members and less than nine members according to the Scrum Guide. There are three key team roles in Scrum. They are the Scrum Master, Product Owner, and Development Team.

A Scrum team should be carefully put together to achieve the advantages offered by the Scrum framework. Scrum teams, much like Agile teams, should be cross-functional. It means that a Scrum team should consist of individuals of different skills and expertise who are required to develop the product without relying on anyone who does not belong to the team.

The team structure in the Scrum framework focuses on the development of small, self-organizing, and cross-functional teams that are flexible, creative, and productive. These independent teams are motivated by the trust that is put upon them to take ownership and get work done. They are trusted to the extent that they directly communicate with stakeholders for feedback.

The Scrum Master

The role responsible for guiding teams to implement the Scrum framework is called a Scrum Master. The Scrum framework is popular as a way to adopt the Agile way of thinking. However, teams require some knowledge and guidance to follow the Scrum framework. Some Scrum practices are often misunderstood and confused with others. Some individuals do not understand the purpose of certain Scrum values. The Scrum Master makes sure that everyone involved in a Scrum project, including the Product Owner, Development Team, and the stakeholders, abide by the Scrum theory, practices, rules, and values.

The Scrum Master plays the role of a servant-leader. The communication between the entities that do not belong to the Scrum team is left to the Scrum Master. The Scrum Master must ensure that interactions between such parties and the Scrum Team are productive and efficient. The Scrum Master is responsible for serving three entities: the company, Product Owner, and Development Team.

The Scrum Master serves the Product Owner by helping the Scrum Team understand the project scope, domain, and goals. He or she must help the Product Owner to manage the Product Backlog by recommending effective techniques. The Scrum Master also must ensure that the Product Owner is focused on maximizing the product's value with the way the Product Backlog is managed.

The Scrum Master must coach and guide the Development Team so that it is self-organizing and cross-functional. Any impediments against teamwork, productivity, efficiency, and Scrum practices need to be identified and eliminated by the Scrum Master. The Scrum Master also has to guide the Scrum Team, especially the Development Team, through Scrum Ceremonies, such as Sprint Planning, Daily Scrums, Sprint Reviews, and Sprint Retrospectives.

A company usually adopts the Scrum framework to develop value-added products while ensuring that projects do not run late or exceed budgets. It is also expected that implementing Scrum helps manage projects with changing requirements successfully. The Scrum Master must ensure that the company can adapt Scrum practices gradually without disrupting productivity and efficiency.

The Product Owner

Scrum is an Agile framework that enables teams to easily adapt to the Agile way of doing things without any prior experience and very little knowledge about the methodology. Therefore, the Product Owner in a Scrum team plays a very similar role that a Product Owner in an Agile environment does.

The Product Owner is responsible for the product's features that the Development Team complete incrementally so that the client can review *Done* versions of the product at the end of each Sprint. One of the Product Owner's key responsibilities is to maintain the Product Backlog. The Product Owner must prioritize items in the Product Backlog after consulting with the stakeholders so that the Development Team picks urgent tasks and features in Sprints instead of low-priority items.

The individuals who play the role of the Product Owner needs to negotiate what Product Backlog items will be completed in a given Sprint. The Development Team usually decides the number of tasks and which ones from the Product Backlog they will complete in a Sprint. The Product Owner can negotiate and agree with the

Development Team to include or drop Product Backlog items from a Sprint.

The Product Owner is equal to any other role in a Scrum team in terms of rank. Many believe that the Product Owner plays a managing role; however, the role is intended to provide guidance to the product that is being developed by the Development Team. The Product Owner represents stakeholders within the Scrum team. Therefore, the stakeholders must respect the decisions that are made by the Product Owner during development.

The Development Team

The group of professionals trusted with the development of the product in a Scrum environment is the Development Team. Since Scrum teams are cross-functional, individuals with varying skill sets and expertise make up the Development Team to complete all aspects of the product development without relying on any external parties. For example, a Development Team that is developing software may include architects, software engineers, business analysts, and testers.

The Development Team collaboratively work on developing *Done* increments of the product until the end product is developed. The Development Team organizes itself. They determine the amount of work they are going to do in a Sprint and what tasks are completed during a Sprint.

The Product Owner can negotiate with the Development Team regarding the items or tasks that are chosen. However, the Product Owner cannot order the Development Team to include or exclude any tasks or items in a Sprint against their will.

The focus on the Development Team is to function efficiently and productively while maintaining a sustainable workload throughout the project. The members of the Development Team need to not only pull their weight but also support the team members since success in Scrum is measured by what the team achieves. As a result, every member of the Development Team is motivated to take ownership and pull their weight during a project.

There are no ranks, titles, or seniority within a Development Team. Every team member is treated equally irrespective of their experience, pay, and area of expertise. Such equality promotes teamwork and increases collaboration within the Development Team.

3.3 Scrum Ceremonies

Some of the key values and principles in the *Agile Manifesto* highlight the importance of face-to-face interactions or meetings between team members, stakeholders, and customers. Scrum is an Agile framework. It puts a similar focus on meetings to maintain efficient and clear communication during projects while avoiding time-consuming meetings and mediums.

Meetings in Scrum are known as *ceremonies*, and they are one of the most important elements of the framework. Scrum's time-boxed and iterative approach uses several ceremonies to maintain Agile practices throughout a project so that a highly satisfactory product is developed. These planned events also aim to increase regularity while reducing unplanned meetings that usually cost time and resources.

Furthermore, Scrum defines maximum durations for ceremonies within the framework. This encourages teams only to spend the prescribed amount of time for each ceremony to improve efficiency. Therefore, events in the Scrum framework have fixed durations depending on the team and the company. Each ceremony is also intended to help teams follow Agile values and principles.

What is a *Sprint* in Scrum?

It is safe to say that Sprints are the most important part of the Scrum framework. They are time-boxed events that should ideally last from one to four weeks. Therefore, a Sprint has a start date and an end date. The duration of a Sprint is determined by the team, depending on the nature of the product being developed. The duration of Sprints usually remains the same throughout a project.

If a complex product is being developed or the product requirements are likely to change quickly, it is recommended that

Sprints should be one or two weeks long. If the product is less complex and unlikely to experience significant change, the Scrum team can opt for Sprints that are three to four weeks long.

Longer Sprints are not ideal since requirements can change during that time. The complexity of changes and risk can also change the longer a Sprint lasts. Therefore, according to Agile values and principles, it is better to make Sprints as short as possible.

One of the key advantages of Sprints is that they provide Scrum teams the opportunity to take a working product to a client for feedback. It ensures that the product they are developing is on track to be the best version of the final product. It also ensures that any changes the client might require can be completed as early as possible, as late changes usually cost more resources.

The end of a Sprint should see the release of a *Done* product increment. This version of the product must be used so that the customer can provide feedback regarding its features and request any changes as they see fit. The end of a Sprint marks the beginning of the next immediately.

A Sprint provides the Scrum team with goals that they work on achieving during the Sprint's length. The Scrum framework recommends that teams do not change the tasks that are agreed upon to be completed during a Sprint once it begins. Doing so usually adds more stress to the team while making it difficult for them to maintain quality. It may also contribute to sustainability issues in the long run, as teams are likely to burn out.

Most teams consider Sprints separate projects. If a Sprint lasts for two weeks, they look at it as a two-week-long project. During this time, several Scrum ceremonies are held. Some are held multiple times, while some only take place once during a specific stage of the Sprint. These events are Sprint Planning, Daily Scum Stand-Ups, Sprint Reviews, and Sprint Retrospectives.

A Sprint may be canceled for a range of reasons. One of the most common reasons is the changing of requirements related to the tasks that have been selected for a Sprint. Changes in technology and the market can also result in the cancellation of Sprints.

Under such circumstances, completing those tasks serves no purpose toward the project. Therefore, the Sprint is canceled, and the team meets to plan a new one. The Product Owner usually decides whether to cancel a Sprint upon consulting the Scrum Master, the Scrum Team, and the stakeholders. If a Sprint is canceled, its goals or the Sprint Goal is considered as obsolete.

When a Sprint is canceled, the Product Backlog is thoroughly inspected to see if the work is releasable. The Product Owner will accept the work if it is releasable. Any incomplete items will be placed back on the Product Backlog to be selected in a future Sprint.

The Scrum framework recommends that Sprint cancellations be avoided. The cancellation of a Sprint usually results in wastage. It also costs additional resources to reassess and move on to a new Sprint. Scrum teams also find it challenging to regroup after the cancellation of a Sprint. As a result, Sprint cancellations are usually rare.

Sprint Planning

This Scrum ceremony takes place at the beginning of each Sprint with the Development Team, Scrum Master, and Product Owner in attendance. The Scrum framework prescribes a maximum duration of two hours for each week in a Sprint. Therefore, if the iteration is two weeks long, Sprint Planning should last four hours or less. If the iteration is for a month, Sprint planning should take a maximum of eight hours.

The Scrum Master has the responsibility to ensure that all the attendees fully understand the purpose of Sprint Planning so that the ceremony is highly productive. The Scrum Master must also ensure that the ceremony does not take longer than the prescribed time and that everything runs smoothly according to Scrum guidelines.

Sprint Planning discussions usually have two core topics. The first includes matters related to what the Development Team intends to complete during the next Sprint. The second includes matters on how the Development Team is going to achieve those goals.

Topic One: Defining Sprint Goals

Sprint Planning organizes the team's work for the next Sprint and sets it on a winning track from the outset. The Product Owner comes into the meeting with a prioritized Product Backlog. These items are then discussed with the Development Team. The Development Team will forecast the amount of work from the Product Backlog that they will sustainably and qualitatively complete. The effort that is required to complete Product Backlog items is estimated collectively by the entire group.

Important factors such as past Sprint performances, the sustainable capacity of the Development Team, and the most recent increment are considered when selecting items from the Product Backlog for the next Sprint. The Development Team needs to take in as much work as possible while committing to completing the work by the Sprint's scheduled end date. They must carefully consider the workload since it is highly prescribed that the workload can be sustained throughout the project without team members burning out.

The Product Owner sometimes converses with the Development Team to make trade-offs. If agreed, certain items that are in the Sprint Backlog are transferred back to the Product Backlog with the agreed Product Backlog items coming into the Sprint Backlog. Therefore, the discussions between the Product Owner and the Development Team can often feel like negotiations.

Topic Two: How to Achieve the Sprint Goals

Once the Scrum Team agrees on *what* they are going to complete in the next Sprint, *how* they will achieve those Sprint Goals is discussed. The items that were agreed to be completed by the Development Team are now transferred to the Sprint Backlog. All the items in the Sprint Backlog need to be completed to a *Done* state by the end of the Sprint.

Discussions regarding how each Sprint Backlog item is going to be completed to a *Done* state are then discussed. The team also draws a plan for the next few days while deciding which Sprint Backlog items will be prioritized. The Product Owner participates in these discussions to provide clarity regarding the backlog items that are being discussed.

There is a likelihood of the Development Team, realizing that they can do more work during the Sprint after these discussions. In such a scenario, the remaining Product Backlog items are discussed and added to the Sprint Backlog. The team then moves on to determining how those items are going to be completed. Upon agreement, the meeting is adjourned, and the agreed Product Backlog items become the Sprint Backlog.

Sprint Goal

One or a collection of objectives for a given Sprint is known as the Sprint Goal. The Sprint Goal should provide some guidance regarding the *Done* increment of the product that will be released at the end of the Sprint. Completion of items that are transferred from the Product Backlog to the Sprint Backlog should allow the Scrum Team to achieve the Sprint Goal. The Scrum Team should identify the Sprint Goal during Sprint Planning so that it motivates them and provides necessary guidance throughout the Sprint.

The Sprint Goal provides the Development Team with an idea regarding the *Done* increment that they are working toward. Therefore, the Sprint Goal keeps the Development Team on track towards completing a successful Sprint. If the Sprint Backlog items are different from the Sprint Goal or do not allow the Development Team to achieve the Sprint Goal, they are renegotiated, and suitable items are added to the Sprint Goal after negotiating with the Product Owner.

For example, if the Sprint Goal is to create the shopping cart of a website. The Sprint Backlog should include items that are related to the shopping cart feature. However, if the Sprint Backlog has items that do not contribute to the completion of the shopping cart, the Development Team needs to renegotiate and transfer Product Backlog items that are related to the shopping cart feature into the Sprint Backlog.

Daily Scrum

Stand-up meetings that take place daily with the attendance of the Product Owner, Scrum Master and the Development Team are known as Daily Scrums. It is recommended that Daily Scrums are held before starting work for the day. Therefore, they usually fall in the mornings unless team members are located in different time zones.

Scrum recommends that Daily Scrums are held while standing up. Sitting down is discouraged since it makes attendees comfortable, which usually results in meetings running longer than required. A Daily Scrum should not last longer than fifteen minutes. It is also customary to hold Daily Scrums at the same location at the same time to maintain continuity.

One of the main purposes of Daily Scrums is to enhance communication, performance, and collaboration among the Development Team. The Development Team answers three main questions during a Daily Scrum: "What did I achieve yesterday?", "What will I work on today?" and "Is there anything stopping me from achieving it?"

The first question takes a look at the previous day while providing the Development Team a view of where they stand in terms of the Sprint Goal. Doing so provides the team with an understanding of what needs to be done to keep on track regarding achieving their goals as a team.

Then the team focuses on what tasks they are going to complete that day. Work is divided among team members as equally as possible. Such self-organizing teams often take more ownership of their work that results in better productivity and efficiency. Any factors that block team members from achieving their daily goals are also discussed at the Daily Scrum.

Teams work collaboratively to find solutions for such obstacles. If any team member needs help, the Development Team usually discusses ways to provide the necessary help. For example, if David needs to finish his work for John to start working on his task, the team may divide both the tasks among David and John or assign a different task for John.

Daily Scrums are usually informal. The way they are held depends on the Development Team. Some teams use discussions while others use questions. It is up to the team to decide how they are going to hold Daily Scrums.

Different team members typically meet after the conclusion of a Daily Scrum to further plan their work since some team members may be working on the same tasks or ones that are connected to each other. The Scrum Master guides the team during Daily Scrums and makes sure that they do not last longer than fifteen minutes. The Scrum Master must also ensure that the Development Team is not interrupted by any others during Daily Scrums even if they are invited to the Development Team meeting.

Sprint Review

The end of a Sprint should see the Scrum Team presenting a *Done* increment of the product to the customer. This occurs during the Sprint Review, where the Development Team, Scrum Master, Product Owner, and the project stakeholders are present. The Product Owner is responsible for inviting the necessary stakeholders to a Sprint Review.

A Sprint Review should ideally last an hour or less for a Sprint that spans a week. The Scrum Master has to ensure that the ceremony does not last longer than ideal. The Scrum Master must also ensure that the purpose of the Sprint Review is understood by everyone present.

The Development Team presents what was achieved during the recent Sprint by showcasing the product's *Done* increment. The project stakeholders, along with the Product Owner, inspect the product increment, and look for any deviations from the Product Backlog items. If any such deviations are identified, changes are requested. The stakeholders can also request changes if original changes have been changed or if they find new ways to add value to the end product.

Many Scrum Teams and stakeholders confuse Sprint Reviews with traditional Status Meetings. Sprint Reviews compared to Status Meetings are highly informal. The emphasis is more on receiving feedback from the stakeholders rather than presenting the project's state and progress. However, the presentation is done so that the stakeholders can provide feedback.

During the Sprint Review, the Product Owner informally lets the attendees know the Product Backlog items that were completed in the Sprint. Then the Development Team lets the attendees know how the Sprint progressed, including the problems that came up and how they solved them.

Then the Development Team presents the product's *Done* increment to the attendees. For example, if the Shopping Cart feature was added to the website, which is the end product of the project, the Development Team will present the *Done* Shopping Cart feature to the attendees.

The stakeholders and the Product Owner may see that the Development Team has not developed the Shopping Cart Summary at the check-out during the presentation. They may request it to be added. Furthermore, the stakeholders may say that they would like to display a new type of tax in the Shopping Card Summary, which may not be a requirement that was captured earlier. Both changes will make it into the Product Backlog.

Therefore, the Product Backlog is likely to be changed during a Sprint Review or as a result of it, with items being added or removed by the Product Owner. The Sprint Review, as a result, should provide the attendees, especially the stakeholders, with an update regarding the project timeline, budget, and the capabilities of the end product.

Sprint Retrospective

Scrum, being an Agile framework, encourages teams to improve as they move from one development cycle to another. Sprints provide teams opportunities to improve both as teams as well as individuals. The Scrum ceremonies that provide teams the opportunity to reflect on their work and improve are known as Sprint Retrospectives.

The Sprint Retrospectives usually take place after the conclusion of the Sprint Review. It is also customary for the Sprint Planning to begin once the Sprint Retrospective is over. A Sprint Retrospective should be no longer than 45 minutes for a week-long Sprint. Similarly, it must not exceed three hours for a Sprint of four weeks. The Scrum Master guides Sprint Retrospectives and ensures that they do not exceed the optimal allocated duration.

Sprint Retrospectives are attended by the Scrum Master, Development Team, and the Product Owner. The Scrum Master must ensure that all attendees understand the aim of Sprint Retrospectives and that the ceremony is productive. It is also important to highlight that the Scrum Master's role is equal to everyone else in the ceremony; however, he or she guides the ceremony.

Sprint Retrospectives are ceremonies that enable teams to reflect on how development went during a Sprint. Individual performances, as well as tools and processes, are openly discussed so that teams can come up with solutions to avoid the repetition of mistakes and improve. The Scrum Team's collaborative performance is also reflected upon at Sprint Retrospectives. Any solutions that are identified will be practiced and applied in the next Sprint.

The Scrum framework recommends that the Scrum Master provides the team with motivation and encouragement to improve continuously so that the next Sprints and future projects run smoothly.

A Sprint Retrospective is adjourned once the team has identified what went wrong and what they will do in the next Sprint to overcome those struggles. However, it is up to the team to decide when and if they are going to implement the solutions identified at a Sprint Retrospective since the ceremony only aims to provide them with an opportunity to reflect and improve.

3.4 Scrum Artifacts

One of the biggest downfalls of traditional project management was the heavy focus on documentation. Agile emerged to reduce documentation; however, some documentation was still recommended to keep teams and stakeholders informed and aligned. Scrum, being an Agile framework, involves less documentation. The documents that aid the management of product development in Scrum are known as Scrum Artifacts.

Product Backlog

This document is a list that includes all the requirements and features of the end product. The Product Backlog items are prioritized so that they can be selected into Sprints accordingly by the Development Team. The Product Owner is responsible for the creation and maintenance of the Product Backlog.

One of the Product Backlog's unique features is that it remains a *work in progress* until the end of the project. The Scrum framework embraces change. Therefore, any changes identified by the Scrum Team or stakeholders are added to the Product Backlog by the Product Owner. Then the list is ordered again.

It is natural for the Product Backlog to be simple at the start of a project. It may only include requirements and features for a basic product. However, the Product Backlog evolves parallel to the product's development. New features, functionalities, requirements, enhancements, and fixes are added to the list along the way, while some items may also be taken down.

For example, when it comes to the development of a website, the Product Backlog may only include the development of the website's basic elements. The completion of the first couple of Sprints may see the Product Backlog being populated with more complex requirements, such as the product and category pages.

Each item listed on the Product Backlog needs to have a description, order, estimate, and value. These include the descriptions that are intended to aid testing. These items may be updated or removed as the product is developed, and feedback is received from the stakeholders.

Some companies may consist of multiple Scrum teams working on the same product. Although multiple products collaboratively develop the same product, only one Product Backlog is maintained. However, items may be grouped so that teams can easily identify the items assigned to their teams.

One of the most important activities involving the Product Backlog is Product Backlog refinement. The Product Owner, along with the Development Team, adds descriptions, priority levels, and estimates to the Product Backlog items. The refinement of the Product Backlog is an ongoing activity where Scrum Teams collectively decide when to do it.

The Scrum Guide prescribes that less than ten percent of the Development Team's capacity should be consumed for Product Backlog refinement. However, the Product Owner can update the Product Backlog and its items at any time. Product Backlog refinement is important since the Scrum Team uses the Product Backlog to understand the end product that is being developed.

Furthermore, the Product Backlog is used to weigh the work that needs to be done to reach the project's end goal. The Product Owner maintains the Product Backlog by keeping track of the work completed and the work that remains. These updates usually take place during Sprint Reviews.

Agile methodology and the Scrum framework both measure progress by the work that has been completed. Therefore, progress is determined by comparing the amount of work that remains between each Sprint. For example, if 500 hours' worth of work remained at the end of the previous Sprint and only 450 hours remain by the end of the current Sprint, the Scrum Team can say that the current Sprint achieved 50 hours' worth of work.

The amount of work that needs to be completed to close the project is calculated similarly using the Product Backlog. Therefore, the Product Backlog acts as a valuable and key Scrum Artifact for the Scrum Team as well as the stakeholders.

Sprint Backlog

The Product Backlog items that the Development Team chooses to complete in a Sprint are populated on the Sprint Backlog. The Sprint Backlog works as a guide for the Scrum Team to achieve the Sprint Goal and release a *Done* product increment at the end of the Sprint. Therefore, the Sprint Backlog can be seen as a forecast of the product increment created by the Development Team, detailing what will be completed in the Sprint and the amount of work that needs to be done to achieve it.

The Development Team uses the Sprint Backlog to guide Daily Scrums. The team discusses the current state of work by assessing the work completed on the previous day and proceeds to make plans for the day. They use the Sprint Backlog to be reminded of the work left to do by the end of the Sprint.

The Sprint Backlog is a *work in progress* similar to the Product Backlog. However, it is the Development Team that modifies the Sprint Backlog. Any new items added as a result of changes are added to the Sprint Backlog by the Development Team. Estimates of the work that needs to be done are updated on the Sprint Backlog every day so that the team is aware of the progress they are making toward achieving the Sprint Goal.

The Development Team can remove any items in the Sprint Backlog that they feel are unnecessary. The Sprint Backlog is a Scrum Artifact that belongs to the Development Team. It is often used by teams to guide them toward achieving Sprint Goals without missing any Product Backlog items that are chosen to be completed in a Sprint.

3.5 A Scrum Example

Peter is assigned to the role of Product Owner of a project that intends to develop a software application. Peter starts his work by gathering requirements and writing down use cases upon having discussions with the customer, other stakeholders, and the architects. Peter goes on to create the Product Backlog for the project after he completes collecting requirements and high-level uses cases.

Peter seeks a few senior developers' help when creating the Product Backlog, especially with prioritizing items and making estimations. At the end of the session, Peter completes the Product Backlog with all the gathered requirements and use cases along with their priorities and estimations.

Now that the high-level use cases have been listed on the Product Backlog and prioritized, Peter begins to break them down into smaller user stories. Once he has broken down enough high-level user stories, he informs the Scrum Master for the first Sprint Planning ceremony.

John, who is the Scrum Master, informs the Development Team regarding the Sprint Planning ceremony. Peter briefs the Development Team regarding the project and goes on to present Product Backlog items starting with the highest priority to the lowest. Then, the Development Team members ask Peter some questions regarding certain Product Backlog items that Peter clarifies.

The Development Team discusses their capacity and whether they have the required expertise to complete the project. After agreeing that they have the experts in the team, and confirming the amount of work they can complete during the Sprint, the Development Team commits to complete Product Backlog stories 1, 3, 4, 5, 7, and 8. Items 2 and 6 are not chosen since they have some technical requirements that are not yet in place. John goes on to adjourn the Sprint Planning ceremony.

Once the Sprint Planning meeting is over, John asks the Development Team to explain how they intend to complete the items that they committed to. The Development Team creates a task board that acts as a Sprint Backlog. Different team members are assigned to complete tasks that are on the board. No other Scrum ceremonies occur for the remainder of the day with the Development Team carrying out their work.

The next day starts with the Scrum Master, John, calling the first Daily Scrum meeting. John asks each individual of the Development Team to let everyone know what they have achieved so far. As each team member provides information about the work that is being achieved, John updates the Task Board with estimations of the remaining hours for each task.

John then asks team members about what they plan on doing for the day. He also asks if any obstacles might keep them from doing their work. Team members briefly explain what they intend to achieve during the day. Most team members do not have any impediments against achieving their goals except for Ross, who seems to have a license issue with one of the software tools he is using.

John asks if any other members of the Development Team have the same issue. Upon checking, he finds out that Molly also has the same issue. John tells them that he will look into the matter. The Daily Scrum is adjourned and only takes thirteen minutes.

John calls the systems administrator and informs him about the license issue Ross and Molly are facing. The systems administrator attends to the problem quickly by purchasing two licenses for them. Upon hearing that the license issue has been sorted out, John checks with Ross and Molly to see if they can work without any issues.

The next day begins with the entire Scrum Team getting together for the Daily Scrum. The meeting progresses well with team members providing updates regarding the work that was achieved the previous day, their plans for the next day, and John updating the Task Board. This Daily Scrum only takes ten minutes.

In a few hours, Kenny is faced with a problem regarding one of the user stories. He heads over to Peter, who is the Product Owner, to ask for clarification. Peter explains the user story to Kenny, who finds the clarity he was looking for. He can carry on with his work without any problems.

The remaining ten days of the two-week Sprint progress without any major incidents. Daily Scrums take place with the Scrum Team being updated regarding the progress of the work.

On the final day of the first Sprint, John calls for a Sprint Review meeting. John also invites Brenda, who represents the customer for the meeting. The Development Team has already prepared a computer with the *Done* product increment to be presented at the meeting. The latest release is presented to the attendees.

Peter, along with Brenda, follows the presentation very carefully, with Peter concluding that the Product Backlog items 1, 4, 5, and 7 have been completed. However, item 3 was not completed on time. Therefore, it was not included in the product increment that was presented.

Furthermore, item 8 needs to be clarified as it is missing some points. Brenda points out that item 5 needs to be slightly changed with Peter taking note. The Sprint Review meeting is adjourned.

John calls for the Sprint Retrospective ceremony a while later, where the team discusses things that went well and what did not during the Sprint. The reasons behind item 3 not being completed are looked into with the team discussing ways to avoid similar mistakes in the future. The reasons behind the team's failure to identify the missing points in item 8 are discussed.

The Development Team mentions that one of the main reasons behind the few downfalls in the first Sprint was due to the lack of understanding of the system architecture. John asks Peter to address this issue. Peter responds by inviting a system architect to take the Development Team through the system architecture. The Sprint Retrospective is adjourned with the team having identified ways to improve. Peter updates the Product Backlog with new items that he gathered after having a discussion with Brenda. Furthermore, he adds the missing points of the user story 8 and updates the Product Backlog. He also adds the changes Brenda requested to item 5.

Peter calls for the Sprint Planning meeting in the morning on the next day. The Development Team discusses user stories with Peter and commits to some under the guidance of John. The Sprint Planning meeting is adjourned, and the second Sprint begins. The

Daily Scrums take place for the next fourteen days. The items that the team committed to are completed without any issues.

At the Sprint Review, Brenda requests a few changes, which are updated on the Product Backlog by Peter. The Sprint Retrospective also concludes with the team hoping to make some minor improvements. Peter calls for the Sprint Planning meeting for the third and final Sprint on the same day. The Development Team decides to complete all the remaining Product Backlog items in this Sprint and commits to them.

The Sprint runs smoothly, with the team functioning well. Daily Scrums take place efficiently with John's direction, while Peter is involved whenever the Development Team requires any clarifications. The third and final Sprint ends with the Development Team completing all the committed tasks successfully.

The final product is presented at the Sprint Review. The customer, Brenda, and the Product Owner, Peter, are highly satisfied with the end product. John calls for the Sprint Retrospective to finally identify the lessons that can be learned from the final Sprint. The project is closed.

Chapter 4: Kanban Method

Kanban, which is spelled "Kamban" in Japanese, is an Agile framework that uses visualization to understand processes and workflows better and actual work done in those processes. Kanban has become popular to identify and manage bottlenecks in workflows so that the work runs smoothly at an optimal speed.

Kamban, in Japanese, means "Billboard," and in Chinese, it means "Signboard." These visual representations are used to indicate the "available capacity to work." Therefore, Kanban is a framework that helps manage processes and workflows by visualizing work. It ultimately helps processes achieve optimal efficiency and adapt to the Agile way of thinking.

Although Kanban is a framework that originated in the manufacturing industry, it became highly popular in the software development world. It has since been used across sectors, especially in the recent past. However, there are many misinterpretations about Kanban as it gains in popularity. Therefore, it is important to understand Kanban correctly before implementing the framework.

4.1 Kanban and Agile

Agile is a project management methodology that can be considered a way of thinking, where projects are broken into more manageable smaller chunks. Highly motivated, self-organizing teams work on those chunks to deliver working increments of the product to receive feedback from the stakeholders along the way. Teams in Agile environments regularly and continuously improve. Agile methodology was first intended to be used in the software development industry; however, it has been adopted by many other industries to manage complex projects with changing requirements.

Kanban, on the other hand, is a method or a framework that agrees with the Agile values and principles. Many companies find Agile somewhat difficult to adopt since it requires coaching and guidance from someone who has knowledge and experience about the methodology. However, Kanban is similar to the Scrum framework as it enables companies to become Agile without requiring much experience and know-how.

Therefore, Kanban can be called an Agile framework. It has many similarities to Scrum, as well as subtle differences. More importantly, Kanban's core philosophy is similar to the Agile way of thinking, just like Scrum. Scrum and Kanban use the visual representation of work by using a physical board or a digital representation of a Kanban board. The work in a Kanban or Scrum project can be divided into three main categories: the work that needs to be done, work in progress, and the work that has been achieved.

The Kanban method is based on the *Kanban Board*, which plays a vital role in helping teams visualize the workflow and progress toward their ultimate goals. Teams can easily understand how different teams complete tasks while they collaborate with the same outcome. Every piece of work at varying development stages are represented on the Kanban Board.

The visual representation of tasks and how they are achieved not only bring transparency and clarity into teams but also helps them identify and manage bottlenecks that they may never have identified. The Kanban method also allows teams to reprioritize work according to their stakeholders' needs, resulting in increased customer satisfaction. Teams are also encouraged to collaborate and strive for improvements by solving weaknesses in their processes.

The Kanban method allows more flexibility when it comes to the tasks that are selected to be completed in an iteration. For example, Kanban does not have a Sprint backlog where only the tasks that are in the Sprint Backlog are completed in a Sprint. Therefore, teams implementing Kanban can work on tasks if they become more urgent while in the middle of a development cycle.

The Kanban method was first applied in software development by David J. Anderson in 2004, almost half a century since its inception in Japan. David was inspired by the works of Taiichi Ohno, Edward Demmings, Eli Goldratt, and many others. He published *Kanban: Successful Evolutionary Change for Your Technology Business* in 2010, which is considered one of the most comprehensive guides to the Kanban Method.

Kanban soon started expanding into other industries. Its focus on gradual improvements within teams that were along the Agile way of thinking was one of the key factors behind its popularity. Kanban is now used in many industries and sectors, including information technology, sales and marketing, recruitment, staffing, and procurement. The principles of the Kanban Method are also so simple and powerful that they could be applied to any business function.

4.2 The Origins of Kanban

The Kanban method goes back decades; however, it is just starting to gain popularity in some industries. The Japanese carmaker, Toyota, stared optimizing and enhancing their processes using a similar model to what was used to stack shelves in supermarkets. The model is based on stocking a similar number of products on the shelves according to consumer demand.

The practice was proven to be successful since inventory levels matched the patterns around consumption. Therefore, supermarkets found it easier to manage inventory. More importantly, they managed to reduce excess stock in their stores that they were responsible for. However, any given product was still available for the customers whenever they needed it.

In the early 1940s, Toyota was not happy with the level of efficiency and productivity in their firms, especially compared to their American rivals. Taiichi Ohno, who was a businessman and industrial engineer at Toyota in Japan, came up with a very simple planning system. The system aimed to control and manage inventory and work at every stage of production.

The system was called Kanban. By implementing Kanban, Toyota managed to increase productivity and reduce costs related to maintaining inventories of raw materials, semi-finished, and finished products. Kanban controls the flow of the product from the supplier to the consumer. As a result, it can help eliminate many costly issues, such as the disruption of the supply and the overstocking of materials and goods during manufacturing.

One of the basic requirements of Kanban is continuous monitoring. Any process that implements Kanban needs to be monitored closely and continuously for it to be successful. Attention must be given to identify and avoid bottlenecks that can potentially disrupt the production process.

Before the application of Kanban, Toyota was dealing with massive overheads relating to inventory levels. There was no systematic relationship with their inventory levels and the requirement of those materials for production. Kanban introduced a visual approach to overcome such struggles where capacity levels in the factory were communicated using Kanban cards.

When a production line in the factory ran out of nuts and bolts, a Kanban was sent to the warehouse with a description of the material needed, the amount needed, and other important details. The warehouse would then issue the exact number of nuts and bolts to the factory line while sending a Kanban to their supplier for the same material and the same amount. Upon receiving the Kanban, the supplier would issue the materials to the warehouse from the stocks.

The Kanban system eliminates the need for the factory floor, warehouse, and the supplier to maintain too much inventory. They only need to maintain just enough to keep production going. Whenever they issue a certain item, a Kanban is sent out requesting for the same amount so that the optimal inventory levels can be maintained to keep production flowing.

4.3 Key Values and Philosophies of Kanban

The Kanban Method prescribes several practices and principles that can be applied to teams to improve their workflow. It is popular for being a highly non-disruptive method to encourage continuous and regular improvements to processes. Kanban principles and practices help businesses achieve better flow in their processes, reduced cycle times, increased predictability, and increased product value. Therefore, adopting the Kanban method is a highly attractive proposition for many businesses belonging to different sectors.

Kanban Principles

The Kanban Method describes several principles that can be easily practiced by individuals and teams to enjoy the benefits that the method offers. These principles are very simple and easy to understand. Furthermore, they are usually unlikely to disrupt a process, making them very easy to adopt.

Start with What You Are Doing Now

Kanban recommends that companies not disrupt the way things are done when adopting the method. The method sees such disruption as negative and disadvantageous. The current processes should be left alone while Kanban is applied directly to the workflow.

Changes to the processes can be done gradually at a pace that teams are comfortable with.

Agree to Pursue Incremental and Evolutionary Change

Making radical changes to a team's process often reduces productivity for a considerable amount of time. As a result, Kanban recommends making smaller incremental changes. The application of radical changes often leads to resistance from teams and employees, resulting in the entire exercise being unsuccessful.

Initially, Respect Current Roles, Job Titles, and Responsibilities

Methodologies such as Agile and frameworks such as Scrum impose organizational changes and changes to the way employees are managed. As a result, many companies struggle to adopt such methodologies and frameworks. Kanban is easy to implement since it does not require any organizational changes.

Existing roles, responsibilities, and the way employees function in their roles are left alone. Therefore, factors that contribute to good performances are left alone. The implementation of Kanban will result in team members implementing required changes without the need to enforce them.

Encourage Acts of Leadership at All Levels

Kanban, being an Agile method, encourages teams to improve continuously. The Kanban method does not limit leadership qualities to specific job titles or roles. One does not need to have seniority or a management role to become a leader when Kanban is applied. Team members at all levels are encouraged to share their ideas so that teams can collaboratively improve as they progress with work.

4.4 The Goal of Kanban

The Kanban Method is a non-disruptive management system that enables processes to be improved using small steps instead of radical changes. Many minor changes are used to improve processes without risking the current processes and causing teams and stakeholders to resist change. Principles and practices in Kanban aim to achieve a set of goals that are highly beneficial for companies.

Planning Flexibility

A Kanban team focuses on the work at hand. They do not commit to new work until the work in progress is completed. As soon as a work in progress task is completed, the item at the top of the backlog is attended to. The Product Owner maintains backlog priority, and any changes to its priority do not affect the work that is in progress.

As long as high priority items are accurately identified, the team automatically ends up committing to them. This results in teams offering maximum value to the company without limiting them to iterations. Iterations often limit teams to a number of tasks that they commit to at the very beginning of it.

For example, a Scrum team commits to several tasks from the Product Backlog to be completed during the Sprint. These items are then added to the Sprint Backlog. The team does not commit to any more items during the Sprint. However, a Kanban team does not limit itself to a certain list of items. Instead, it focuses on finishing the work at hand. As soon as the work is complete, the task with the highest priority is taken from the Product Backlog. Therefore, the Kanban Method offers better flexibility when it comes to planning.

Shorter Time Cycles

One of the key metrics for Kanban teams is Cycle Time. It refers to the time that a unit of work takes to travel from the moment the development starts until it is shipped out. Optimizing cycle time makes the team more productive and enables them to forecast how quickly products can be delivered correctly. The Kanban Method aims to shorten cycle time by overlapping skill sets through mentoring and knowledge transfers.

Reducing Bottlenecks

The more items that are in progress, the more teams need to multi-task, and the longer it takes for those items to be completed. As a result, the Kanban Method focuses on limiting the work that is in progress. Work in Progress Limits can be used to highlight bottlenecks within a process as well as backups that are usually caused by a lack of people and skillsets.

Visual Metrics

One of the Kanban Method's core values is to continuously strive for improvements so that teams become increasingly efficient and effective. Teams respond well to visual metrics, such as charts, where they can see improvements visually and become motivated. Kanban teams use cumulative flow charts and control charts as visual metrics to identify and eliminate bottlenecks, resulting in improved processes.

Continuous Delivery

The Kanban Method focuses on continuously delivering working increments of a developed product. For example, when a Kanban team is developing the software, they are focused on building code for a particular item, testing the code, and releasing the item once it is done so that the customer can use the feature and provide feedback.

4.5 Implementing Kanban

The Kanban method has gained popularity across various sectors as it is easy to apply to processes and setups. It clearly describes what needs to be done to avoid disruptions to processes and cause resistance within teams. The six core practices explained in Kanban are aimed toward the implementation of Kanban successfully without inducing negative resistance disrupting the performance of teams.

The Kanban Method aims to increase project performance by visualizing the workflow while encouraging teams to improve continuously. It also enables the customer to be more involved during the development phase of a project, just like other Agile frameworks. However, Kanban also has some features that are different from many Agile frameworks.

Most Agile frameworks feature iterations that last a certain period and involve multiple tasks. However, a development cycle in Kanban is the time taken for a single user story to go through all the stages of work in a process until it is marked as *Done*. Therefore, implementing the Kanban method can be tricky for some companies. Patience and gradual changes may be required when implementing the Kanban method.

Step 1: Visualize the Flow of Work

The first fundamental step toward adopting the Kanban Method is to visualize the steps in the process currently being used to develop a product or service in a company. Visualization of the steps can be done physically, with the use of a Kanban Board, or digitally, with the use of a digital tool that represents a Kanban Board. Kanban Boards representing different processes can look different. Some may look simple, while others may be very complex, depending on the processes that they represent.

Different types of cards and colors can be used to highlight the significance of different work items. Kanban Boards also feature Swim Lanes, where each lane is dedicated to a particular type of work item. However, the Kanban Method recommends that things be kept simple initially while focusing on gradual changes. Therefore, a single Swim Lane may represent the entire process in the beginning with the possibility of gradual redesigning of the representation down the road as teams become more comfortable with the visualization of the processes.

Step 2: Limiting *Work in Progress* (WIP)

This practice encourages teams to finish the tasks that are at hand or *in progress* before committing to new ones. Therefore, the work that is currently marked as *Work in Progress* first needs to be completed and marked as *Done* before taking up new work. This practice results in the efficient use of the capacity within teams. They end up completing work and taking up more work at a faster pace.

It is natural for teams to struggle when it comes to initially determining their WIP limits. Therefore, it is recommended that Kanban is implemented with no WIP limits in place. The work in progress is first observed, and limits are only applied after analyzing substantial data. Most teams typically start with a Work in Progress Limit of between one to 1.5 times the number of team members contributing to a specific stage. Introducing WIP limits to columns in the Kanban Board helps team members finish what they have at hand first before committing to new work. Furthermore, it also provides transparency—since stakeholders, including the customer, can see that the team's capacity is limited. This encourages them to plan their requests and manage their expectations.

Step 3: Managing Flow

Once the first two practices are implemented, managing and improving the flow begins. It is a difficult practice to implement, and it must also be done carefully. Now that the workflow has been defined and Work in Progress Limits have been carefully set, there should be a smooth flow within those WIP limits or work should start piling up. The workflow needs to be adjusted so that it is improved, depending on how it flows upon applying the first two principles.

One of the key ways of achieving this goal is by carefully observing the workflow to identify bottlenecks. Attention must be given to intermediate wait stages where work items that are marked as *Done* are handed off. Reducing the time that *Done* items are parked in these intermediate work stages results in eliminating bottlenecks and reducing cycle time.

As improvements are made gradually, teams begin to deliver work smoothly and more predictably. When predictability improves, it is easier to make commitments to customers and their requests without taking the risk of disappointing them. Improving the accuracy of forecasts regarding product completion times is one of the main advantages that the Kanban method offers.

Step 4: Making Process Policies Explicit

Just like processes are visualized explicitly, the Kanban Method recommends that policies or rules and guidelines are made explicit. These policies decide the way teams work, and making rules and guidelines overtly encourages everyone who takes part in those processes to work the same way. They will know how to work in any situation according to the rules and guidelines that are made very clear.

Processes may have different policies at different levels or stages. They may exist in specific Swim Lanes or specific columns. They may involve a checklist that dictates entry or exit criteria for a certain column. Making policies unambiguous helps processes run smoothly without irregularities. Therefore, policies need to be made explicit and represented visually on the Kanban Board for each Swim Lane and column.

Step 5: Implementing Feedback Loops

Any good methodology, framework, or system emphasizes feedback loops. The Kanban Method helps organizations implement different kinds of feedback loops. These include reviewing different stages in the workflow, reports, and metrics, as well as visual clues that provide feedback regarding the workflow that needs to be implemented. Feedback needs to be taken early, especially when things are not going great, so improvements can be made. Feedback loops are critical to make those improvements and deliver a satisfactory product or service to the customer.

Step 6: Improving Collaboratively and Evolving Experimentally by Using the Scientific Method

The Kanban Method enables companies to gradually improve their processes and workflows without posing difficulties to those involved in the processes. The use of the scientific method is encouraged to make those improvements and evolve through experimentation. A hypothesis is first formed, followed by tests. Changes are then made according to the outcomes of those tests.

When the Kanban Method is implemented, there needs to be continuous evaluations and improvements based on those evaluations. The Kanban system makes it easy to experiment since it provides signals to help teams figure out if a change is helping them improve.

Chapter 5: Lean Thinking

Most companies that have been in operation for a few decades or even more still run with the same processes and setups that were put in place decades ago. Some processes may have been left untouched since the company started operations. Many business owners believe that they can use the same process over decades simply because they work. It may look true and practiced at a glance. After all, why fix something that is not broken?

However, the problem with such an approach toward using the same decades-long processes is that the world of business is continuously evolving. There may be rare instances where leaving processes as they are is the wisest choice. However, generally, most businesses need to evolve with the world that they belong to.

Take the hospitality industry, for example. People may have checked-in casually to a hotel at the front desk where all the gathering of details, payments, security deposits, customer reviews, and complaints may have been carried out. The front desk handled all those tasks decades ago. Today, the front desk is still capable of handling all those tasks. It can even handle a range of tasks much quicker compared to those days. However, most of those tasks do not make it to the front desk.

Most customers search for hotels over the Internet. They may provide some or most of their details when making a reservation, and they may also pay in advance electronically. Most customers will leave reviews and complaints online after their stay. Therefore, the front desk has become less important; however, it can get things done just as it did decades ago.

Imagine if a hotel decided to solely rely on the "front days" like the good old days just because it works. Imagine a hotel not providing online reservations, payments, reviews, and complaints in modern times. The chances are that most guests will not even know about the hotel.

Therefore, most businesses need to evolve alongside the world, industry, technology, and consumer behavior to remain successful. Competition keeps increasing, and newer players enter markets with innovative solutions. The businesses that have been around for a long time need to continuously challenge themselves to improve and fine-tune their processes.

Lean Management focuses on reducing and eliminating waste. Various industries have used the teachings and philosophies of Lean starting from the manufacturing industry and going as far as the software development industry. Companies have been able to increase productivity, eliminate waste, and improve quality using Lean Management. However, the business world is still discovering the true value and power of Lean Thinking and Lean Management.

Lean Management reduces waste and focuses on adding value to products and services that are being developed. Therefore, Lean is a set of tools and techniques that can be used to reduce waste and add value to different processes. However, it must be noted that the definition of Lean may slightly vary depending on the industry, country, region, or even the company it is implemented in. For example, Lean is considered a mindset or a way of thinking instead of a set of tools and techniques.

History of Lean

When it comes to the origins of Lean, Toyota rings bells in many people's minds. However, it must be noted that the roots of Lean Thinking go back to fifteenth-century Venice. The concept of Lean was successfully used in manufacturing by Henry Fort in 1799. The groundbreaking concept of interchangeable parts was also introduced by Eli Whitney the same year.

In 1913, Henry Ford came up with an idea to experiment with the flow of production in the application of interchanging parts. The purpose was to standardize work. However, Ford's system was limited in use since it lacked variety. It was only applicable to one specification. Nevertheless, an important stride was made.

Shiego Shingo and Taiichi Ohno, working for Toyota, invented the Toyota Production System in the 1930s. Shiego Shingo and Taiichi Ohno were inspired by Henry Ford's theory relating to the flow of production. Toyota's systems aimed to reduce the cost of production, improve the quality of products, and enhance the throughput times to meet dynamic customer requirements.

John Krafcik first introduced the term "Lean" in one of his articles in 1988, titled "Triumph of the Lean Production System." The article explained how Lean manufacturing was used in various plants to achieve higher quality and productivity levels compared to traditional manufacturing processes.

He also highlighted that the technology that was being used in different plants did not affect performance levels. Furthermore, Krafcik noted that any risks associated with the implementation of Lean could be reduced by better training, flexibility in the workforce, easy-to-build product designs, high-quality products, and an efficient network of suppliers.

Lean Thinking soon became popular in the manufacturing industry. Recently, Lean Thinking has been used in Software Development with great success. Furthermore, Lean has spread into several sectors, including healthcare, with an increasing number of companies starting to use Lean practices.

5.1 Lean Principles

Lean describes five principles that act as a framework to help businesses improve the efficiency and effectiveness of their processes. Lean helps managers identify inefficiencies in their process and steps in processes that do not offer any value to the customer. Lean Thinking encourages businesses to create better workflows where continuous improvement is made part of the culture. A company can be highly competitive, increase the value offered to clients, decrease production costs, and increase profits by practicing the five principles of Lean.

1. Define Customer Value

It is important to understand what value really is to understand the first principle of Lean Thinking. Value in Lean Thinking refers to the value of the product the customer is willing to pay for. Therefore, it's important to understand the exact requirements of the customer. Some features may add value to the product. However, the customer may not be willing to pay for those features for a variety of reasons.

The customer may not understand the value of those features. He or she may not have the budget. Irrespective of the reasoning behind a customer's unwillingness to pay for a feature that may add value to a product, it's important to understand what customers value and not—failing to do so results in high production costs and reduced profits.

For example, a camera can be developed with a feature that enables the user to upload a video to YouTube with a single press of a button. However, most customers may not be willing to pay extra for such a feature. Therefore, adding that feature to the product may not be profitable; nevertheless, it is surely useful and convenient.

2. Map the Value Stream

This principle focuses on identifying activities that contribute to values relating to the customer's definition of value. Any activity that does not contribute to offering value to the end customer is considered as waste. Such activities are broken down into two categories in Lean Thinking: non-value but necessary, and non-value and unnecessary.

A company should try to reduce the former as much as possible. However, non-value and unnecessary activities should be eliminated as they are pure waste. The reduction of the first category and elimination of the second usually leads to the development of a product that matches the value the customer is willing to pay.

3. Create Flow

The removal of activities that are considered waste and reducing activities that do not add value but are necessary can disrupt processes differently. Therefore, it is important to ensure a smooth flow of the remainder of the steps so that there are not any delays or interruptions in a process. Activities that can be used to create flow include the reconfiguration of the production steps, the breakdown of those steps, making the workload more even, the creation of cross-functional departments, and the training of multi-skilled and adaptive employees.

4. Establish Pull

One of the biggest wastes in any production system is inventory. This principle aims to limit inventory and items, and are WIP (work in progress) so that the current stock of materials and resources remain available for a smooth workflow. This principle encourages businesses to develop products at the time they are required, and in the exact quantities that are required.

Pull-based systems use the needs of customers to direct them. The customer's exact needs are determined, and the value stream is followed backward through the production system. It ensures that the products that are developed will satisfy the needs of customers instead of going to waste.

5. Pursue Perfection

The application of the first four principles reduces and eliminates waste. However, the fifth principle is considered the most important as it encourages businesses to chase perfection. Lean Thinking does not encourage businesses to relax once they achieve a smooth flow with minimal waste. Instead, it encourages companies to nurture a culture where teams continuously seek ways to improve. In such an environment, employees actively seek perfection with their activities. The company, its teams, and employees continue to learn with their processes, improving and evolving bit by bit every day.

5.2 Eight Wastes of Lean

Lean is a way of thinking focused on removing wastes from processes while adding value to products. Therefore, it is important to understand what is considered waste in Lean. Lean Thinking defines waste as any step in a process that does not add any value to the customer. Simply put, waste is a process that the customer doesn't find useful or is not willing to pay for.

1. Transport

Waste produced during transportation includes the movement of workers, tools and equipment, inventory, and products any further than necessary. Unnecessary movement can often lead to damages and defects of tools, materials, and products while putting workers at the risk of injury. It also results in unnecessary work, exhaustion, and costly wear and tear.

Waste in transportation can be reduced by placing workers who collaborate near each other. The materials and tools necessary for production must also be easily accessible by workers without unnecessarily moving around. Double or triple handling of materials should be eliminated. Many businesses use proper planning of production lines, using U-shaped production lines, enhancing the flow between processes, and avoiding the over-production of WIP (work in progress) items.

2. Inventory

Many businesses rarely think about excess inventory as waste. In a financial sense, bulk purchases allow businesses to be entitled to discounts, while inventory is considered as an asset in accounting. However, having more inventory than the necessary amount to maintain a steady flow of work usually leads to various problems, including damaged materials, product defects, increased lead times, unnecessary spending on inventory, and unidentified problems hidden in inventory.

Inventory waste can be many things depending on the business. In an office environment, it may be files that are waiting around to be worked on or records in an unused database. Broken machines, additional finished products, and extra materials occupying workspace are considered inventory waste in manufacturing. Inventory wastes can be reduced by only purchasing raw materials when needed, purchasing the required quantities, reducing buffers, and creating queues to eliminate overproduction.

3. Motion

Any movement of people, machinery, and equipment that is considered unnecessary is wasted motion. It includes unnecessary walking, reaching of all kinds, and physical movement to reach other workers, tools, and products. Tasks that may involve a lot of motion may be redesigned so that unnecessary motion is reduced as much as possible while paying close attention to health and safety standards.

In an office environment, the wasted motion includes activities such as reaching for materials like files, walking to a cupboard that stores files, unnecessary mouse clicks, and entering data twice. In manufacturing, activities such as reaching for materials and tools, walking to access materials and tools, and readjusting components after installation are examples for wasted motion.

Wasted motion can be reduced significantly by redesigning and organizing workstations, proper placement of equipment close to the workers who need them, and the placement of materials in ergonomic positions so that reaching for them is unnecessary.

4. Waiting

Any unnecessary waiting is considered waste. It includes workers waiting for raw materials and equipment, machinery and equipment that are idle, and workers waiting on other workers to finish work. Uneven production stations and flaws in processes often cause such wastes. In an office environment, waiting for waste may happen as workers wait for emails from coworkers, as workers wait for files to be reviewed, and the time wasted in ineffective and unnecessarily long meetings. Waiting for waste can be reduced by redesigning processes so that there is a continuous flow, making workloads more even by standardizing work instructions, and the development of multi-skilled workers who can quickly adjust to the demands of the work.

5. Overproduction

When a product or part of a product is developed before it is required, the result is overproduction waste. Businesses are often tempted to produce extra products so that they are available when required. They may see it as beneficial since workers and machinery are rarely left idle.

That type of production is caused by "Just in Case" thinking, which is the opposite of Lean Thinking. Overproduction results in increased storage costs, defects being unidentified due to the large amount of WIP—preventing smooth workflow—and increased lead-time.

In an office environment, making extra copies of files, the creation of reports that do not serve a purpose or interest others, providing unnecessary information and details, and doing a service available before the customer is ready are overproduction waste. Ensuring that the rate of manufacturing is even between stations—single-piece flow or manufacturing small batches—and the use of the Kanban Method to control WIP can usually reduce overproduction waste.

6. Overprocessing

Doing more work than necessary, adding unnecessary components to products, and adding features and steps in a product that are not required by the customer are considered as overprocessing waste. In manufacturing, the use of equipment that is unnecessarily expensive, using parts that have capacities beyond requirements, unnecessary analysis, and readjusting components after they have already been adjusted are some examples of overprocessing waste. In an office environment, the creation of reports that have too much detail, processes that involve too many steps, having unnecessary individuals sign certain documents, and having unnecessary forms are overprocessing waste examples.

Overprocessing waste can be reduced by looking at the work requirements from the customer's viewpoint. The customer should be in mind when designing and adjusting processes and workflows. Workers should also be encouraged to reflect on whether the customer would see value in each of their actions and if the customer is willing to pay for their work.

7. Defects

Products that are not fit for use are known as defects. Defects are usually reworked or scrapped. Reworking results in considerable waste since additional resources are required to bring a product to a usable state. Scrapping results in a total waste of time and resources spent on that product. Therefore, both results are wasteful as they do not deliver any value to the customer.

Defects can be countered by identifying common defects in a process and addressing those issues. Redesigning of processes so that they do no create products with abnormalities is one of the best ways to eliminate defects. However, there is always a likelihood of a defected product being developed; therefore, processes should be improved so that such products are identified before they reach the end customer.

8. Skills – The Eighth Waste

The eighth waste defined in Lean Thinking was not a part of the Toyota Production System. The eighth waste describes unused and misused human talent. This type of waste usually occurs when businesses separate the management of the processes from the actual workers. Managers are responsible for planning, controlling, organizing, and innovation. Meanwhile, employees are required to follow orders and do the work that managers plan and organize.

In such circumstances, the expertise and knowledge of frontline workers are wasted, and opportunities to improve processes are lost. People who actually do the work often have a better understanding of the processes in place and how they can be achieved. Therefore, they need to be encouraged to come up with solutions and ways to improve processes in a company instead of limiting them to "work."

In offices, poor incentives, insufficient training and coaching, ignoring employee feedback, and placing employees in roles below their qualifications, skills, and experience usually result in the wasting of skills. In manufacturing, skills are wasted when workers are not provided with adequate training to operate machinery and equipment, provided with unsuitable tools to carry out a certain job, and when workers aren't challenged enough to improve and come up with ideas to improve processes.

5.3 Lean Management

Lean Thinking is becoming increasingly popular among companies belonging to various sectors. As a result, there are many success stories where the implementation of Lean Thinking has helped companies reduce waste and increase profits while continuously improving their processes.

FedEx Express

This company is known throughout the world for delivering airmail and packages. The company maintains a sizable fleet of aircraft and ships that help transport cargo throughout the world. Aircraft maintenance is one of the main operations at FedEx Express that costs resources and space.

The global recession in 2008 forced FedEx Express to resort to Lean Thinking in a bid to save money during those difficult times. The focus on reducing waste and continuous improvements may have resulted in the decision to adopt Lean Thinking.

Before implementing Lean Management, the FedEx facility at the Los Angeles International Airport (LAX) managed to complete fourteen C-Checks per year. C-Checks are a type of aircraft maintenance checks. After implementing Lean principles, the maintenance crew at the same facility managed to complete thirty C-Checks per year. Prior to the adoption of Lean Thinking, it took the

FedEx crew around 32,000 working hours to complete a single C-Check. However, the adoption of Lean Practices cut this time significantly, with the crew only needing an average of 21,000 working hours per C-Check.

One of the key reasons behind the drastic changes was the identification of milestones. The team identified 68 milestones that needed to be completed to complete a C-Check successfully. Doing so enabled them to make the workflow smoother while reducing waste considerably.

Nike

The athletic fashion label is one of the most popular businesses to benefit from the implementation of Lean Thinking. Nike has benefited by adopting Lean Management and continues to reach new levels of productivity and waste reduction year after year thanks to Lean Management.

The year 2012 was a special year for Nike as it released its first FY 10-11 Sustainable Business Performance Summary. It was the first Manufacturing Index released by the label. The FY 10-11 introduced several quality standards that would be practiced across Nike's numerous factories located all around the world.

These explicit policies and guidelines increased consistency between different factories while reducing miscommunications and misunderstandings common before the release of FY 10-11. Setting clear expectations brought consistency to Nike's processes across factories and increased the overall performance and quality of their processes. Furthermore, CO_2 emissions of factories declined by six percent during the time while production increased by twenty percent.

5.4 Lean and Agile

Both Agile and Lean are flexible methods focused on helping teams develop high-quality products sustainably while making gradual improvements. Both methods emphasize the importance of providing high-value products for customers delivered in short iterations instead of a single, long development cycle.

Agile and Lean share numerous values and principles. However, Agile and Lean are not the same; however, many individuals wrongly believe that they are. Therefore, some teams that practice Agile or Lean do not have a clear understanding of the similarities and differences between them.

Agile or Lean can be considered a good influence; however, they are most beneficial when implemented holistically. Failure to understand them often leads to unsuccessful implementations that do not bring the results that many companies hope to achieve.

Approach to Speed and Iteration

Agile teams aim to deliver usable software at regular intervals. Such releases often begin when the development is at an early stage. Early and regular releases enable teams to use valuable feedback from customers and adapt to change with ease.

Lean Management also has a similar principle where teams are encouraged to deliver fast. The faster a team can deliver value to their customer, the quicker they will get feedback from them. The difference between the Agile and Lean principles is that in Lean Thinking, teams increase the speed of delivery by limiting work-in-progress items. However, in Agile, teams rely on smaller development cycles to deliver working product increments quickly.

Customers First

Lean and Agile both encourage teams to focus on customer satisfaction as one of their primary goals. Agile teams ensure customer satisfaction by starting an early and continuous dialog with customers and facilitating changes that add value to products that are being developed. Customers are more involved in the development process and usually end up receiving a product that is full of value.

Lean teams focus on the customer by providing the customer with what they are willing to pay for. Lean Thinking considers anything that the customer is not willing to pay for as waste. Therefore, customers are likely to get exactly what they ask for instead of products with missing features or additional features that they do not find useful.

Role of Discipline

Agile recommends more structured teams and roles compared to Lean Management. Agile relies on defined roles, various estimation techniques, defined roles, systematic reviews, and many other project management practices. The disciplined nature of Agile processes allows teams to develop products faster and embrace change well.

Lean Thinking relies on discipline, but in a different way. Lean Thinking is successful when it becomes a part of a company's culture. Lean Thinking does not require teams to uphold external rules and expectations. It is more about every individual and team upholding Lean principles in unison.

Conclusion

Traditional project management methodologies that existed by the dawn of the twenty-first century were linear and sequential. These attributes resulted in projects running late, while teams struggled to deal with the later identified changes. The Agile Alliance that met in a ski resort in Utah in 2001 released the *Agile Manifesto* that described four values and twelve principles aimed at resolving issues that the software development industry faced at the time.

The values and principles of Agile focused on small, self-organizing, and cross-functional teams working on small increments of products that enabled customers to be more involved during a project's development phase. Customers would be provided with working product increments from an early stage in development. Each regular increment would give customers the chance to provide feedback and request changes.

The Agile philosophy recommends that teams embrace change instead of avoiding it. Change is inevitable in many projects due to failures in requirement gathering and analysis and quickly evolving market and customer needs. As a result, a methodology that can respond to change positively was welcomed by the software development industry. Agile soon became highly popular in IT firms while spreading to other industries, from healthcare and construction to marketing and sales.

While many companies realized the benefits that the Agile methodology offered, one of the main reasons for adopting Agile was the need for expertise and knowledge. Agile principles and values were difficult for teams to grasp, especially for those who had followed traditional project management approaches for years. As a result, the need for Agile frameworks with clear steps and guidelines emerged.

Scrum is an Agile framework that enabled organizations to become Agile without needing prior Agile experience and knowledge. Scrum provided clear guidelines on how to form teams, specific team roles and responsibilities, types of meetings or ceremonies that would help practice Agile values and principles, and several Scrum artifacts to guide documentation to lead teams toward project goals.

Kanban is a method that involved the visualization of workflows and processes with the use of Kanban Boards. The concept originated in the factories of the Japanese carmaker Toyota, while the Kanban Method was later introduced so that businesses across different industries could utilize it to improve team performance with the visualization of processes and workflows. The Kanban Method has many similarities to the Agile methodology, including striving for continuous improvements within teams and processes, among many.

Lean Thinking is another approach that has many similarities to the values and principles described in the Agile way of doing things. However, Lean Thinking and Agile are not the same methodology or approach. Lean Thinking focuses on achieving optimal productivity and product value by reducing and eliminating waste in processes. Lean identifies eight types of wastes along with five principles that guide teams to reduce and eliminate waste while continuously making gradual improvements to the way they work.

The Agile methodology has helped many teams achieve project goals through true collaboration. Its openness to change has made it one of the best methodologies for projects with varying requirements and evolving needs. Scrum is a framework that guides teams who are willing to adopt Agile values and principles. Similarly, Kanban and Lean are methods that can ensure the smooth flow of processes while eliminating waste and bottlenecks.

All these methodologies, frameworks, and approaches offer various advantages and disadvantages to businesses. Some of them may be more or less suitable for companies, teams, and projects. Therefore, it is important to clearly understand their values and practices, so the best methodology or framework can be chosen to manage a project.

Here's another book by Robert McCarthy that you might be interested in

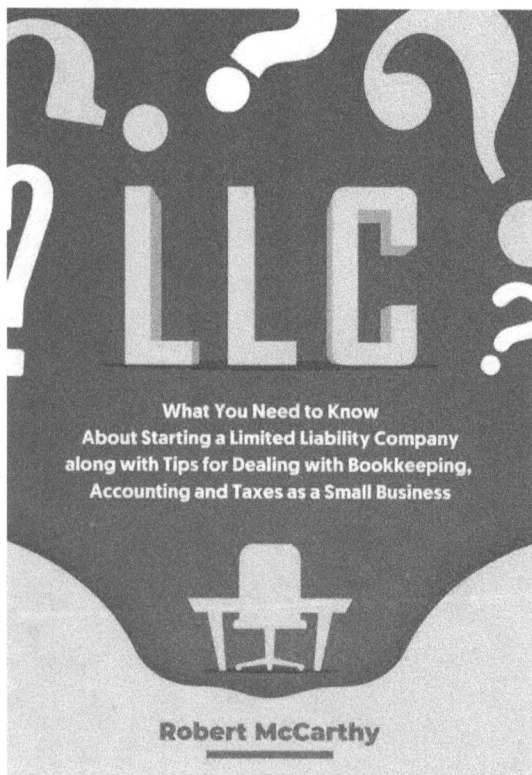

LLC

What You Need to Know
About Starting a Limited Liability Company
along with Tips for Dealing with Bookkeeping,
Accounting and Taxes as a Small Business

Robert McCarthy

www.ingramcontent.com/pod-product-compliance
Lightning Source LLC
Chambersburg PA
CBHW050645190326
41458CB00008B/2424